Mark practised in major commercial law firms for thirty years, specialising in property dispute resolution. He has acted for businesses large and small, including FTSE-listed property companies and household-name corporate occupiers, across the whole range of property-related issues.

He is now a full-time commercial property management law trainer, putting his expertise and experience to good use in training both lawyers and surveyors. He delivers training both in-house and for providers including MBL Seminars, Professional Conferences, CPT Events and Solicitors Group. Mark is also the author of a number of books within his areas of expertise.

# Short-Term Commercial Lets for Lawyers, Agents, Landlords and Tenants – A Practical Guide

# Short-Term Commercial Lets for Lawyers, Agents, Landlords and Tenants – A Practical Guide

Mark Shelton
MA (Hons) Law (Cantab), Non-Practising Solicitor
Commercial Property Management Law Trainer
www.marksheltontraining.co.uk

Law Brief Publishing

The information in this book was believed to be correct at the time of writing. All content is for information purposes only and is not intended as legal advice. No liability is accepted by either the publisher or author for any errors or omissions (whether negligent or not) that it may contain. Professional advice should always be obtained before applying any information to particular circumstances.

Published 2021 by Law Brief Publishing, an imprint of Law Brief Publishing Ltd
30 The Parks
Minehead
Somerset
TA24 8BT

www.lawbriefpublishing.com

Paperback: 978-1-913715-19-9

# PREFACE

The average duration of new commercial leases being granted at present is historically very low, and has been for some years. This trend has been amplified and accelerated by the Covid-19 crisis. There is increased demand for pop-up, flexible lettings in many sectors.

One of the challenges this presents is keeping transaction costs down. A landlord who grants a 25-year lease has one set of letting costs in 25 years, and will be very ready to pay commercial solicitors to draft and negotiate a comprehensive lease, which may well run to 70 pages or more. If, instead, the landlord lets the property for a succession of three-year terms over the same period, it faces eight sets of costs, and will be reluctant to incur professional fees which might add up to some months' rent, on each occasion.

Another priority for landlords in relation to such short-term lettings has conventionally been to avoid the tenant benefitting from security of tenure. The tenant it is prepared to accept for two years may not be the tenant it would accept for a longer period, and the terms of such a lease are likely to be different from what they would be in relation to a longer term. The landlord will not want to see the arrangement extended into an indefinite future.

Those two objectives have often been achieved by the use of short-form, standard 'licences to occupy', signed without any involvement of solicitors, though the use of this form of agreement is not without risk. To avoid the risk, sometimes a 'tenancy at will' may be used instead, although that option has its own pros and cons. The safest option to avoid security of tenure is a short-term lease, contracted-out of the Landlord and Tenant Act 1954. However, many agents and landlords are resistant to that, believing that it cannot be done without involving lawyers, and will therefore be too expensive.

One of the aims of this book is to demonstrate that that need not be the case. It is not the intention to encourage landlords or tenants to prepare or negotiate leases without professional assistance. There are risks for the tenant in doing without the detailed investigations which a solicitor would undertake, and there are risks for both parties in negotiating the terms of the lease themselves.

However, one cannot ignore the reality that landlord and tenants will increasingly document lettings on a DIY basis, whether professional advisers believe it to be wise or not. Standard forms of short-term commercial lease, promoted by reputable professional bodies, are available for free on the internet, and it is easier than ever before for the agent or lay person, with some knowledge and common sense, to document a contracted-out lease for themselves. This book aims to supply the necessary knowledge.

That does not mean there is no role for the solicitor. While a solicitor may not always be retained to draft leases, the selection of a standard form which will be acceptable, and the development of protocols for the execution of leases and the conduct of the contracting-out process, are areas in which solicitors can add value. Moreover, certain processes are reserved by law for solicitors, and there are 'here be dragons' areas into which the lay person should not stray. The solicitor can signpost these pitfalls.

This book will consider the available options, including the content of three standard lease forms, and the parameters within which agents and landlords can document lettings with confidence. Where solicitors are retained to document leases in the traditional way, it will assist in doing that economically.

The first four chapters of the book are concerned with explaining the key content of commercial leases, and are written with the lay person principally in mind. This part includes a glossary of useful terms, and also a step-by-step guide for the non-lawyer.

The remainder of the book is concerned with how to document a short-term commercial letting. It builds on the earlier content for the benefit of the lay person, but is intended also to provide useful guidance for the property professional, whether letting agent, surveyor, or lawyer.

This book states the law as it was on 25 January 2021.

Mark Shelton
February 2021

# CONTENTS

# PART ONE

# AN INTRODUCTION TO THE CONTENT OF LEASES – FOR LANDLORDS AND OCCUPIERS

Part 1 of this book, Chapters 1 – 4, is concerned with explaining the key content of commercial leases, and is written with the lay person principally in mind. It includes a glossary of useful terms, and a step-by-step guide for the non-lawyer.

Part 2, Chapters 5 – 10, will be concerned with how to document a short-term commercial letting. It will build on the earlier content for the benefit of the lay person, but is intended also to provide useful guidance for the property professional, whether letting agent, surveyor, or lawyer.

# CHAPTER ONE

# WHAT MUST I PAY?

**This chapter outlines the principal financial obligations under commercial leases.**

While there are a considerable number of Acts of Parliament which regulate the landlord and tenant relationship, the most important source of the parties' rights and obligations is the terms of the contract, i.e. the lease.

## The journey away from the 'institutional lease'

Thirty or forty years ago, commercial leases were typically granted for a 25-year term. Tenants would be responsible for the repair of the entire structure, from foundations to roof. The landlord would insure the building, but the tenant or tenants would reimburse the insurance premiums.

This is sometimes referred to as an 'FRI lease', the initials standing for 'full repairing and insuring'. In this model of lease, all the risk of fluctuation in the property overhead is thrown onto the tenant, leaving the landlord a clear rent, hence another common name for it: the 'clear lease'.

This was the dominant commercial lease form, and it was developed by and for property investors, to be a relatively straightforward investment vehicle. It was attractive to institutional investors such as insurance companies and pension funds (hence yet another name for this type of lease: the 'institutional lease').

As regards the rent, under this model of lease it would be reviewed every five years, and could only ever go up, or stay the same. The level of rent would never reduce, even though the rental market might have fallen in the meantime. Security of income over the 25-year term was underpinned by the rule of 'privity of contract', under which a tenant remained liable to pay the rent and perform all the other tenant's obligations despite having transferred the lease to someone else. The transferee would in turn be bound in the same way, after having transferred the lease again, and so on, so that as time went on the landlord stood to accumulate an ever-growing list of parties against whom the lease terms might be enforced.

A lease following that template was not obviously a good deal for tenants, and much has changed since then, partly as a result of legislation, partly as a result of self-regulation initiatives within the property industry, but mainly as a result of the market turning in tenants' favour over a long market-cycle.

The average length of new lease terms has been falling for years, and has been at or around five years for some time. In a lease of that length, or shorter, there may be no rent review. Repair obligations are often now more limited, and there may be a cap on service charges. Break clauses feature in leases regularly, allowing tenants to terminate the lease early. The old 'privity of contract' rule has been abolished.

In this and the next three chapters we consider the key content of commercial leases. In many respects that content owes much to the institutional lease, and it is still routine to speak of a lease, or a specific lease provision, as being 'institutionally acceptable'. However, that template may often now be departed from in important respects.

## Obligation to pay rent

The most fundamental of the tenant's obligations in a lease is to pay the rent. The lease will often require that it be paid by direct debit or standing order, or by bank transfer. It is usual for it to be paid in advance, rather than in arrears.

One consequence of payment in advance is that if the lease comes to an end in the middle of a rental period (actually, on any day other than the *last* day of a rental period) an issue arises as to whether a lesser, proportionate amount is payable on the final rent day prior to the end of the lease. For example, if rent for the period 29 September to 24 December would ordinarily be payable in advance, on 29 September, but it is known that the lease will come to an end on 10 October, is the tenant entitled to pay, on 29 September, a lesser amount calculated for the period up to 10 October? If not, and a full quarter's rent must be paid, is the landlord then obliged to refund, after the lease has come to an end, an amount calculated for the period following 10 October?

The answer to either question is not fixed in law, but depends upon what the lease says.

Rack rent leases

The traditional pricing structure is what is known as a 'rack rent', meaning simply that the tenant pays the full open market rental value of the property. However, in the case of leases for long terms (say, 99 years or more) it would be conventional for the tenant to pay a 'premium', that is a capital sum, in the same way as one would if buying a house. There will usually be a rent payable as well, but this is more as a 'badge' of a lease than anything else, and it will be a nominal amount, sometimes "a peppercorn". This is not encountered that often, since commercial leases are rarely that long. They are typically on a rack rent basis.

In commercial leases, it is unusual for the rent to be expressed as anything other than an annual rate, though of course rent falls due for payment more frequently than once a year. The rent payment days have conventionally fallen quarterly, though monthly payment days are encountered now more often than previously, and monthly payment is usually better for a tenant's cashflow. Where payment is monthly, the lease will of course specify the day of the month on which it falls due. Where it is quarterly, leases very often provide for payment on 'the usual quarter days', which are 25 March, 24 June, 29 September and 25 December (historically, significant dates in the Christian calendar). More modern leases may instead specify 1 April, 1 July, 1 October, and 1 January.

As mentioned above, modern leases are often so short that there is no provision for the rent to be reviewed. Where a lease does contain a rent review clause, it is still usual for it to provide that the review process is upward-only.

## Turnover rent leases

Not all leases are on a rack rent basis. In certain economic sectors, principally retail and hospitality, the value of the premises to the tenant can be assessed very directly by reference to the sales achieved there. An alternative model is therefore for the rent to be calculated, at least in part, on the tenant's turnover.

The usual structure is that the tenant pays a 'base rent', typically around 80% of the open market rental value, plus a percentage of its turnover as a top-up. For tenants who have a very simple business model, and for short leases, landlords are increasingly prepared to agree to a turnover-only arrangement, where there is no base rent, and the tenant simply pays a percentage of its turnover to the landlord.

Where there is a base rent, it will be paid quarterly in advance, just as in a rack rent lease. Calculating the turnover, and paying the turnover-based rent, is administratively more complicated, and of course it cannot be known or paid in advance. With many retailers operating online as well as at bricks and mortar premises, and with increasingly ingenious and innovative ways of generating income being devised all the time, capturing all the turnover referable to a store can be very challenging.

The knock-on implications of a turnover-based rent for the other terms of the lease are surprisingly wide-ranging, and these arrangements can be dauntingly complex. Nevertheless, tenants are often attracted to the idea that the landlord will be taking on some of their business risk, and that their property overhead will have some downward adjustment in difficult trading circumstances. Turnover rents are increasingly common in the retail and hospitality sectors, particularly in the light of the Covid-19 crisis.

## Service charges

If a landlord lets an entire property to one tenant, the expectation is that the tenant will bear the entire cost of repair of the building. If on the other hand the building is, say, an office block which is let in parts to a large number of tenants, things have to work differently. Each tenant will be responsible for the upkeep of their own part of the building; the landlord will be responsible for the repair of the main structure and roof, plant and equipment for heating, air-conditioning etc., also lifts and escalators, and other 'common parts' such as landings, lift lobbies, reception areas and communal toilets. However, the sums spent by the landlord in repairing those elements will be charged to all of the tenants through their individual contributions to a service charge. The end result, from the landlord's point of view, should be exactly the same, in financial terms, as if it had let the whole building to one tenant, responsible for the repair of the entirety.

Service charges will, moreover, allow the landlord to recoup expenditure on other matters, not just repair. That might include the cost of heating and lighting, promotions and advertising, provision of security services, managing agents' fees, and so forth.

In terms of payment mechanism, the most common arrangement is for the landlord or its managing agents to produce a budget for service expenditure on an annual basis, and for the tenant to pay quarterly instalments determined by the amount of the budget. At the end of the service charge year, the landlord prepares accounts showing the actual expenditure on services over the year. Either the tenant is required to pay an additional charge, if the quarterly payments have fallen short of the actual expenditure; or, if they have exceeded it, the landlord may be obliged to make a refund of the overpayment (though it is more common for the amount to be credited against the next year's service charge instead).

Service charges are a common flashpoint between landlord and tenant. The landlord is apt to feel aggrieved if it cannot recover in full the sums expended on providing services for the tenants, while for tenants the service charge mechanism looks suspiciously like a blank cheque. However, it is hard to find a satisfactory alternative.

First, there is a simple practical necessity: an obligation to repair and maintain common parts such as foundations and roofs cannot sensibly be divided up between tenants. Secondly, tenants may be sceptical as to whether the landlord will provide services to the required standard, if not underwritten by the ability to recover the cost from the tenants.

So both parties know they have to live with service charges; but that does not mean that they are not sometimes hotly disputed, especially as compliance with environmental and other requirements continually raises new heads of expenditure on multi-let properties. Tenants may sometimes succeed in negotiating a cap on their annual service charge contributions, which gives some degree of control over the cost.

Service charges for residential property are subject to extensive legislation. As regards commercial property there has been no such statutory regulation. There is, however, a code of practice applying to commercial service charges. The *Code of Practice: Service Charges in Commercial Property* published by the Royal Institution of Chartered Surveyors ("the RICS") was first launched in 2006, and since 1 April 2019 it has been incorporated into the RICS' professional conduct framework in the form of the *RICS Professional Statement on Service Charges in Commercial Property*. It addresses provision of information when the lease is being negotiated, when services are being purchased and provided, and when the service charge is demanded. It makes recommendations as to the content of service charge provisions, and as to the provision of services, and financial management of the service charge.

As it is a Professional Statement, the RICS will take account of its provisions when deciding whether a member has acted professionally and with reasonable competence and it is also likely to be taken into account in court proceedings regarding the competence of surveyors.

## Insurance

Leases invariably provide for landlords to insure the building. This is because it is thought that tenants will be inclined to buy cheap insurance which does not give the comfort the landlord requires. If the landlord insures, it can be certain that the relevant risks are covered, and that the insurer is a reputable and financially sound one. In accordance with the idea of the 'clear lease', though, the tenant will be required to reimburse the insurance premiums.

## "Reserved as rent"

The rent may often be referred to in the lease as 'the Main Rent' or 'the Principal Rent', while service charge and insurance premiums may also be said to be "reserved as rent", or "payable by way of additional rent". Alternatively, they may be called something like "Service Rent" and "Insurance Rent". It is common to find that other sums payable to the landlord too, like reimbursement of professional fees, and interest on rent paid late, are "reserved as rent".

Historically, there were two main purposes of this. One is to do with forfeiture (that is, termination of the lease by the landlord, on the ground that the tenant has breached its lease obligations). This can be done by simply changing the locks to the premises, though generally speaking the tenant must be given a warning notice, and time to put right the breach of the lease. However, no warning notice is required, and no time need be given, where the breach is non-payment of rent.

The other, and more important, reason was that landlords used to enjoy the right to use a procedure known as 'distress for rent'. This enabled them to recover any arrears of rent by instructing bailiffs to go to the property and seize and sell tenants' goods found on the premises. This could be done without warning and without having to go to court, and so it was a very effective and relatively quick and cheap process for landlords. From the tenant's point of view, of course, it appeared to be an unnecessarily aggressive and harsh measure. It could only be done in relation to rent, and so it became normal for leases to describe all sums due to the landlord as different heads of rent. Distress for rent was replaced in 2014 by Commercial Rent Arrears Recovery ("CRAR"), which is a much more regulated and restricted procedure. It cannot be used without prior warning, and it can only be used in relation to rent properly speaking, not service charge or insurance premiums or anything else.

The replacement of distress for rent by CRAR means that the landlord does not gain much of an advantage by having all sums due under the lease described as rent, but it is still very common to see this in leases.

## Other bills

Of course, the cost to the tenant of running the property is not confined to the sums due to the landlord. Business rates is a large expense, potentially as much as 50% of the annual rent. Services such as heating, lighting, water and telephone may also have to be paid for.

### Inclusive rents

As well as turnover rents, another model which is increasingly finding favour is the 'inclusive rent'. That is, the tenant pays only the fixed amount of rent. The landlord may provide services and insurance, the landlord may have responsibility for repair of the premises occupied by the tenant as well as any common parts, and the landlord may even pay the business rates, but none of these costs are recouped from the tenant. It is the opposite, or the negative image, of the clear lease. It gives the tenant certainty as to the amount of its property overhead, and for this reason it is attractive. However, the rent will be higher than it would be if the tenant were bearing these costs.

### Summary

**Rent is usually payable in advance, by equal quarterly instalments. If the lease is of sufficient length, the rent may be reviewed at intervals, and may go up as a result.**

**Rent is usually at the full open market rental value, called a 'rack rent', though in some retail and other leases it may be calculated at least in part by reference to the tenant's turnover, so that the amount fluctuates.**

**Other amounts that tenants must usually expect to pay are service charge, insurance premiums, business rates and other outgoings. So-called 'inclusive rent' is sometimes seen, where the rent is a fixed amount, and no additional charges of those sorts are payable. They are borne instead by the landlord.**

# CHAPTER TWO

# HOW LONG WILL THE LEASE LAST FOR?

**This chapter considers matters relating to the duration of leases.**

When a landlord grants a lease of a property, it hands over possession of that property to the tenant. It will naturally want certainty as to when the arrangement is going to come to an end, so that it can enjoy possession again itself. That may mean that the lease lasts for a fixed period, as is common, or there may be more flexibility built in, but in that case there must at least be a mechanism for terminating the lease. That predictability of when, or at least how, the lease is going to come to an end is regarded by the law as an essential element of what goes to make up a lease, and is referred to as the lease 'term'.

## 'Lease' and 'tenancy'

It is useful at this point to make an observation on terminology. The words 'lease' and 'tenancy' are often used more or less interchangeably, but to be precise, a 'tenancy' is the legal relationship of landlord and tenant, which may be created by a document called a 'lease'. A tenancy may be created in other ways, though, in some cases by oral agreement. It used to be widespread practice in the field of residential lettings that the tenant would be provided with a 'rent book', in which payments were recorded, and that would be the only written evidence of a tenancy. That practice is now largely obsolete, but not completely. A tenancy can also arise in circumstances where there is no agreement at all, but a tenancy is nevertheless said to be 'implied by law'.

One type of tenancy which is much more commonly found in relation to residential premises is a 'periodic tenancy'. A periodic tenancy is a recurring arrangement, and might typically be on a weekly, monthly, quarterly or annual basis. A monthly periodic tenancy, for example, is regarded technically as a tenancy for a month. When it comes to an end, though, another tenancy for a month will come into being automatically, without the parties needing to do anything or sign anything. At the end of that month, another month's tenancy will automatically arise, and so on. The arrangement can be brought to an end by either party giving notice, which is a mechanism that renders the duration sufficiently certain to qualify as a tenancy. This type of arrangement is always called a 'tenancy', and one would never encounter the term 'periodic lease'.

Because periodic tenancies and rent books have historically been common in the residential sphere, it is much more usual in that context to speak of 'tenancies' than 'leases' (except in relation to a lease for a very long fixed term), and the common forms of document are usually called 'tenancy agreements'. In the commercial world, by contrast, where the norm is an agreement for a fixed term, the convention is to refer to the document as a 'lease'. Periodic arrangements are occasionally encountered in relation to commercial property, though, and they are called 'periodic tenancies' just as they are in the case of a residential letting.

## The lease term

In the commercial property world, while leases for 200 years or more may be encountered, these are relatively unusual, and most lease terms will fall into a range between six months and 40 years. As covered in Chapter 1, average lease terms used to be around 25 years, but this has fallen over the last two or three decades, to around five years.

It can be crucial to be precise about the commencement and termination dates, and this can be surprisingly difficult. For example, does a lease term "for five years from 25 March 2020" include that date or not? Conventionally, that form of wording would be interpreted as *not* including 25 March 2020, but that is always subject to other indications elsewhere in the lease or in the surrounding factual background. It is useful when the lease says something like "for five years from *and including* 25 March 2020".

Often the date on which the parties enter into the lease will be the first day of the term, but it need not be. For example, the lease may be signed and dated on 20 April 2021, but it may say that the term begins earlier than that, on 25 March 2021. When a term is backdated in this way, it is for the purpose of calculating the amount of the initial rent payment, and it does not mean that the parties were actually in a landlord and tenant relationship before 20 April; that would be absurd. The case of *Shaw v Kay (1847) 1 Ex. 412* confirms that the tenant only becomes the tenant once the lease is completed.

Another possibility is that the lease is post-dated. The lease might be signed and dated on 20 April 2021, but specify the term commencement date as 24 June 2021. That might be because the tenant already has a lease of the same property from the same landlord, which is going to come to an end on 23 June 2021, and they both want to get a new lease in place ahead of then, so that there will be certainty that the landlord and tenant relationship will continue.

As mentioned above, one does occasionally encounter 'periodic' tenancies of commercial premises. Commercial periodic tenancies are often annual, though the period of recurrence may be shorter (or indeed longer).

Another sub-type of tenancy is the so-called 'tenancy at will'. Tenancies at will may be used with the very specific purpose of preventing the tenant from acquiring security of tenure (which will be dealt with next), and otherwise they are not very suitable to commercial occupation. The nature of a tenancy at will is that it lasts 'at the will' of both parties. In other words, it lasts as long as both parties want it to last, and it is brought to an end, immediately, by one party notifying the other that it is at an end. That is obviously a very precarious sort of relationship, which is why it is rarely suitable. The term length in that arrangement is effectively indefinite, but it is nevertheless regarded as a tenancy. That is explained on the basis that there is at least a minimalist mechanism for termination, in that it is brought to an end by one party telling the other so.

**Security of tenure**

It is convenient to begin this consideration of security of tenure with a quick point as to the different types of tenancy just identified. A periodic tenant *always* has security of tenure, so long as they are in occupation for business purposes. A tenant at will *never* has security of tenure. There is nothing that the parties can do, in either case, to alter that. We are concerned in this book, though, with fixed-term leases, and the parties to a fixed-term lease have the flexibility to decide whether the tenant has security of tenure or not.

Having noted that, we turn to consider what is meant by security of tenure, and how and why it came about. Bombing during the Second World War left a legacy of destroyed properties, residential and commercial, and reconstruction took years. The resulting prolonged shortage of property, by a simple application of the law of supply and demand, put landlords into a strong negotiating position. When leases came to their end, tenants who would not or could not pay an increased rent demanded by the landlord, would have to find other premises, potentially losing goodwill built up over many years at their existing premises. Residential tenants already enjoyed strong protections under the Rent Acts, but protection for business tenants was introduced in *Part II* of the *Landlord and Tenant Act 1954*.

This is the single most important piece of legislation in the field of commercial landlord and tenant law. There are several other Landlord and Tenant Acts, but when people refer to 'the Landlord and Tenant Act', it is always the Landlord and Tenant Act 1954 that they mean. Similarly, it may often be referred to as 'the 1954 Act', or even just 'the Act'.

It applies to business tenancies. Broadly that means anything that is not residential, and it includes uses that one might not think of as 'business', such as schools and sports clubs. (There are specific exclusions for agricultural tenancies and mining leases).

When a tenancy which is within the Act comes to its expiry date, it does not come to an end, but simply continues on all the same terms indefinitely, unless and until either the landlord or the tenant takes action to bring it to an end in one of the ways permitted by the Act. When they do so, the tenant is generally entitled to a new tenancy. That is why the procedure under the 1954 Act is called 'lease renewal', and people may refer to a 'renewal lease', meaning a lease granted as a result of this procedure.

The landlord does have the opportunity to contest the grant of a new lease, on one or more one of seven statutory 'grounds of opposition' set out in the Act. These include matters such as the tenant being in breach of its obligations, for example the repair obligation, or the landlord intending to carry out a redevelopment of the property. Whichever ground of opposition the landlord chooses to rely upon, it has to be proved in court.

The landlord may have to pay compensation to the tenant if it proves its ground of opposition – that depends on which ground of opposition it is. If, for example, the tenant is denied a new lease because it is in breach of its repair obligation, then it has only itself to blame, and will not receive compensation.

Assuming that there will be a new lease, though, as is generally the case, the next question is what it will say. If the parties cannot agree on the terms of the new lease, then the matter is referred to the county court. The court fixes the new lease terms in accordance with the requirements of the Act. The rent will be whatever is the open market rent for the premises at that time, so neither landlord nor tenant will have an unfair advantage; for most other terms, the starting-point is the terms of the old lease, and any party who wants to change those terms must convince the court that there is a sufficiently good reason to do so. The upshot is that lease terms tend to be largely reproduced upon renewal.

The 1954 Act thus removes a landlord's control over (i) the identity of the tenant, (ii) the ability to get possession back, and (iii) the terms of the lease. Nothing about the Act is good news from the landlord's point of view, which is only to be expected, since the Act was passed to protect tenants. That said, the commercial letting market understands and is familiar with the 1954 Act, and the impact is 'priced-in'.

However, there will be occasions where it is important for the landlord that the tenant should not have security of tenure, for example where it intends to redevelop the property at the end of the lease, and wants to have certainty about getting possession back cheaply, instead of having to prove its intention to redevelop under the Act, which is expensive and uncertain.

Of particular relevance in the context of this book, landlords will often want to avoid security of tenure where the letting is for a short term. As observed in the Foreword, a tenant who is acceptable for a two-year term may not be acceptable for a longer commitment, and the terms of a short-term lease are likely to be different from what would be expected in relation to a longer term. The landlord may therefore not be willing that the tenant should acquire the statutory right to have the arrangement continue over a longer period.

On the other hand, landlords currently face a very difficult letting market, particularly as regards retail properties, and may consider that a tenant with security of tenure is likely to remain in occupation, paying rent, for longer. Equally, tenants in the current market may consider that the benefits of flexibility, and of being able to negotiate renewal of their lease against a looming deadline at which they may walk away from the property, make it preferable that they should *not* have security of tenure.

It should be emphasised that these are unusual considerations arising from present economic circumstances, and that the more usual view is that:

- for landlords, security of tenure is best avoided in short-term commercial lettings; and
- for tenants, the 1954 Act confers valuable and important rights, and they should think long and hard before deciding to take a lease without them.

As mentioned above, the parties to a fixed-term lease can, in effect, choose whether or not security of tenure should apply: there are a number of ways in which occupation can be documented so that it does not, which will be considered in Chapter 6. The one which gives greatest certainty is that the lease should be 'contracted-out' – in other words, the parties agree that the relevant parts of the 1954 Act will not apply to it.

There is a procedure which must be followed in order to do that, which is dealt with in Chapter 8.

**Break options**

A break option is very simply a right to bring a lease to an end ahead of what would otherwise be the expiry date, by serving a notice. A lease might be granted for a term of ten years, for example, but with a right to terminate it halfway through, at the end of the fifth year. A break option may be something which can be operated only by the tenant, or only by the landlord, or it may be mutual.

Break options are used for a variety of different reasons.

- Often break options are used just as a means of compromising between the different aims of landlord and tenant for the term length. The landlord may want to grant a ten-year lease, and if the tenant only wants five, then one way of solving the problem is for the lease to be for ten years, but with a break after five years. This has been increasingly common, with the downward trend in the length of lease terms.

- Sometimes the break option is linked to a rent review, so that the tenant has the chance to walk away from the property if it is unhappy with the level of the reviewed rent.

- For a tenant, a break option obviously gives useful flexibility as regards the length of its lease commitment.

Where a tenant serves a break notice, the landlord is faced with a period of time, perhaps a lengthy one, before a new tenant can be found, and a new lease put in place. During that time it will receive no income from the property, and will have to cover all the outgoings. Landlords may well wish to challenge the exercise of break options, therefore, and the law gives plenty of scope to do so.

First, the required formalities must have been complied with correctly. The notice must have been served by the deadline set out in the lease. It must correctly identify the landlord and the tenant. It must be sent to the correct address, and by the correct method.

The other main problem for tenants is that the lease will often set out conditions which must be complied with if the break is to take effect. Compliance with conditions can usually only be assessed at the break date.

A usual condition is that all the rent must have been paid up to date. As mentioned in Chapter 1, this can include payment of a whole final quarter on the last rent day, even though the effect of the break may be to bring the lease to an end mid-way through the quarter. (There may be express terms in the lease to the contrary, though – it is necessary to check).

Some leases make the break conditional on all payments of any kind under the lease being up to date, not just the rent. It can be extremely difficult for the tenant to be sure that this condition has been complied with, and the standard of compliance is strict – every penny must have been paid.

Another usual condition is that the tenant must have given vacant possession. If they still had workmen in the property after the break date, for example, finishing off some repairs, that would be enough to defeat the break option. They might leave a sufficient quantity of their goods or fixtures in the property to interfere substantially with the landlord's use and possession, and that too would be considered a failure to give up vacant possession.

A very problematic condition for tenants is that all repair obligations should have been complied with. The courts apply a very strict standard to this; there was a well-known case in which a break was defeated because the tenant had decorated the property with only two coats of paint where the lease required three. It can be very difficult for tenants to comply with conditions of this sort.

All of these problems can be avoided in the wording used in the lease. The *Lease Code*, discussed in Chapter 5, is helpful to tenants on this point, as are the three standard forms of lease considered in Chapter 9.

## Summary

**The law requires that the length of a lease (its 'term') is certain: it must be a fixed period, or there must be a mechanism for identifying an end date, such as giving a notice. Commercial leases are rarely less than six months or more than 40 years. The term commencement may be back-dated to before the lease is executed, or it may be post-dated to begin at some time after the date of execution.**

**Periodic tenancies are recurring arrangements, which usually run on a monthly, quarterly or annual basis. A tenancy at will lasts only as long as both parties want it to, and is terminated immediately by one party notifying the other that it is at an end. Fixed-term tenancies are much more common than either of these.**

**A fixed-term lease may be protected by security of tenure under the *Landlord and Tenant Act 1954*. This means that the tenancy will not terminate on the date that it says it will, but will continue unless and until terminated by the procedures set out in the Act. When that happens, the tenant usually has the right to a new lease, on controlled terms, unless the landlord can prove one of a number of statutory grounds for opposing the grant of a new lease. Depending on which ground is relied upon, the landlord may have to pay the tenant compensation for the non-renewal of its lease.**

**The parties can, however, agree that those protections will not apply to a lease. In order to do so effectively, they must first comply with a statutory procedure. This process is called 'contracting-out'.**

**Tenants can have greater flexibility as to length of term if the lease includes a 'break clause', allowing early termination upon service of a notice. Exercising such break rights can be difficult in practice, though the difficulties can be very much reduced by the lease drafting.**

# CHAPTER THREE

# FOR WHAT ACTIONS MUST I HAVE LANDLORD'S CONSENT?

**This chapter deals with how landlords retain control over properties by means of prohibiting certain actions, unless done with landlord's prior consent.**

In principle, when a property is leased, it is the tenant's to do with as it wishes during the lease term. In the case of a long residential lease, granted perhaps for a 999-year term at a peppercorn rent, the landlord has, to all intents and purposes, disposed of the property completely, and one would expect it to have only minimal control over what the tenant does.

In the case of a typical commercial lease, however, granted for a term possibly as short as six months, and seldom for a term longer than 40 years, the landlord retains a significant interest in the property. It will be mindful of the fate of the property after expiry of the lease term, and will want to have it back in a condition that keeps open all options as to re-letting, selling or perhaps redevelopment. In other words, it wants to preserve the value of its investment. It is a priority that the tenant in occupation should be of sufficient financial substance to comply with its obligations as to payment of rent, and the repair and insurance of the property. Equally, the landlord will be concerned to limit the permitted business uses of the property, as well as what alterations may be made to it.

On the tenant's part, it will want freedom to deal with the property in whatever way it considers most beneficial to its commercial activities. That may simply be a matter of what sort of business it is permitted to conduct at the property; it may be a matter of reconfiguring the property, or installing specific facilities or equipment; or it may be a matter of disposing of the property, if it has become surplus to requirements or uneconomic to run.

The objectives of landlord and tenant will not necessarily conflict, but the lease drafting must anticipate the possibility that they will, and the usual means of providing for that is to prohibit certain actions by the tenant, unless the landlord gives its prior consent to any such action. The process of obtaining consent (if the tenant), and considering, often resisting, the grant of consent (if the landlord), is a recurring flashpoint in the landlord and tenant relationship.

## Types of prohibitions in leases

Prohibitions fall into different classes: they may be absolute, qualified or fully qualified.

- An absolute prohibition does not contemplate any consent by the landlord, but simply bans the action outright. That is not to say that the landlord may not be persuaded to consent to the prohibited action regardless, however such a 'consent' would in reality amount to a variation of the lease terms. The landlord's discretion as to whether to grant or refuse consent in such a case is absolute.

- Under a qualified prohibition, the action may not be undertaken *unless the landlord gives its prior consent.*

- Under a fully qualified prohibition, the action may not be undertaken unless the landlord gives its prior consent, *not to be unreasonably withheld.* The usual form of words is 'not to be unreasonably withheld or delayed', but where the words 'or delayed' are omitted, a sufficiently lengthy delay can of course amount to 'withholding' anyway.

Absolute and fully qualified prohibitions are routinely encountered in leases, when dealing with the main areas of restriction: dealings with the property (principally assignment of the lease or sub-letting the premises), alterations and use. Qualified prohibitions are comparatively rare.

## Typical restrictions

### Alienation

Dealings with the property may include assignment, sub-letting, charging, holding on trust, and parting with or sharing possession or occupation. Collectively, these types of dealing are referred to as 'alienation'. There will usually be quite detailed and lengthy provision in a lease dealing with alienation.

This may be a crucial issue for the tenant, if it needs to offload premises because it is making a loss, or because much better premises have become available. For the landlord, it is no less crucial to be satisfied that the occupier of the premises has the means to pay the rent and keep the property in repair, and that no unacceptable use of the premises is proposed.

Alienation clauses typically begin with a comprehensive prohibition of any kind of dealing whatsoever. This prohibition usually applies both in relation to the whole of the premises, and in relation to part of them, and will be expressed as an absolute prohibition. However, it will be subject to exceptions, as provided for in the remainder of the clause.

- There will generally be an exception permitting assignment of the lease as a whole, with the landlord's prior consent, not to be unreasonably withheld or delayed. There may be specific circumstances set out in the clause in which the landlord will be entitled to refuse consent (for example the proposed assignee does not meet some financial test), or conditions which the landlord will be entitled to impose upon any consent (for example provision by the proposed assignee of an acceptable guarantor). Assignment of part of a lease, while theoretically possible, gives rise to difficult technical and practical problems, and so is usually excluded from the scope of this exception; it is therefore absolutely prohibited.

- Sub-letting is usually dealt with in some detail, and whether sub-letting of part is permitted will depend largely upon the nature of the property. A tenant whose lease comprises five floors of an office block may well be permitted to sub-let individual floors (sometimes half-floors, depending on the configuration of the building). A tenant of a light industrial unit, on the other hand, will probably not be permitted to sub-let in part, since the property may not be easily divided.

Insofar as sub-letting is permitted, whether in whole or in part, there are usually pre-conditions: typically, a proposed sub-letting may only be allowed, by way of exception to the general absolute prohibition, if: (a) it is to be at the best market rent obtainable; (b) it is to be otherwise upon all the same terms as the lease; and (c) it is to be contracted-out of the *Landlord and Tenant Act 1954*. Provided all those pre-conditions are met, sub-letting is permitted with the landlord's prior consent, not to be unreasonably withheld or delayed.

- There are sometimes arrangements for groups of companies, whereby sub-letting to companies within the same group as the tenant is permitted, without any requirement for a specific consent. Parting with or sharing occupation or possession is sometimes also permitted to group companies, again without any specific consent.

*s.19(1), Landlord and Tenant Act 1927*, applies to transform any qualified prohibition on assignment or sub-letting into a fully qualified one. The effect is to make it rare to see an alienation restriction in the qualified form. It will be either absolute (i.e. the lease makes no mention of landlord's consent) or fully qualified (i.e. landlord's consent cannot be unreasonably withheld).

## Alterations

The wording of the alterations clause will depend upon the type of building and the extent of the property which is let to the tenant. A lease of whole will typically permit the tenant to carry out a broader range of alterations than a lease of part. In a lease of part, structural and external works are often not permitted at all, and this is sometimes the case with a lease of whole. A tenant of a stand-alone industrial unit will expect to have more flexibility than a tenant of a unit in a shopping centre. Different landlords have different policies as well.

These different outcomes are achieved by distinguishing between different categories of alteration.

- Certain types of work may not be prohibited at all, being permitted by a blanket permission in the lease. A lease of office premises, for example, might permit the installation and removal of demountable partitioning, while a warehouse lease might permit the installation and removal of full-height racking. Sometimes the permission is expressed more broadly, to allow any internal non-structural work. So long as the tenant's proposed work falls within this category, specific consent is not required, although there is normally a requirement to notify the landlord after the works have been carried out.

- At the other end of the spectrum, there is generally a category of work which is absolutely prohibited. This is likely to include structural work, and may perhaps extend to matters affecting the external appearance of the property. That may be important where the building is listed, or is in a conservation area, or simply for maintaining the visual unity of a development.

- The third, residual category is alterations which are subject to a fully qualified prohibition, i.e. work which can only be carried out with the landlord's prior consent, not to be unreasonably withheld or delayed.

*s.19(2), Landlord and Tenant Act 1927,* like *s.19(1)* in relation to assignment or sub-letting, turns any qualified prohibition on alterations into a fully qualified one so, again, it is rare to see an alterations restriction in the qualified form. It will be either absolute or fully qualified.

Use

The use clause in a lease sets out the permitted use of the property, and usually prohibits all other uses. There is generally also a restriction on any use which may cause nuisance or annoyance to neighbouring occupiers, and some leases specifically prohibit use for illegal or immoral purposes.

The prohibition on all but the permitted use is generally an absolute one, so that questions of landlord's consent rarely arise. There is no statutory provision to the effect that consent must not be unreasonably withheld, either. Retail leases, though, may contain a fully qualified, or sometimes just a qualified, prohibition. A lease might provide for a specific use such as the sale of ladies' fashion clothing, while permitting any other retail use with landlord's consent, not to be unreasonably withheld or delayed. In such a case, a change to anything other than another retail use would fall within the absolute prohibition.

Planning controls

There will normally be a separate clause governing whether the tenant is permitted to make planning applications, which may be needed before tenants can make alterations or change the use of premises. The landlord will be concerned that a breach of planning law by the tenant could lead to enforcement action against the landlord, and potentially have an adverse impact on the investment value of the property.

Usually the lease will provide that the tenant will not apply for, or implement, a planning consent without the landlord's consent, not to be unreasonably withheld or delayed so long as the landlord has consented to the activity underlying the tenant's application for planning consent (i.e. alterations or change of use). There may also be a provision that if the tenant implements a planning consent, it will comply with any conditions, and implement the consent in full, before the end of the term. The landlord's concern is that if the tenant leaves a consent only partly implemented, the local authority could require the landlord to complete the implementation after the lease has ended.

As regards use, the permitted use of the property will fall within one of the Use Classes set out in the *Town and Country Planning (Use Classes) Order 1987*, and indeed the use clause may well define the permitted use by reference to one or more such Use Class. Change from one Use Class to another generally requires planning permission, though some shifts between Use Classes are permitted by the *Town and Country Planning (General Permitted Development) (England) Order 2015.*

It is important to bear in mind that the two restrictions, contractual and statutory, are parallel and unconnected. If a change of use from one Use Class to another is permitted by the planning legislation, it may still be prohibited by the use clause in the lease, and the planning position will not necessarily determine whether a landlord's refusal to permit change of use is reasonable or not.

The Use Classes were radically liberalised in 2020, partly with the aim of rejuvenating struggling high streets, in response to the difficulties experienced as a result of the Covid-19 pandemic. That means that planning authorities now have much less control over change of use, and in turn the lease provisions are all the more important.

## Summary

**There are various actions which a tenant may wish to carry out, which are usually prohibited in leases, or can only be carried out with landlord's consent, so as to preserve a degree of control over the property for the landlord.**

- **Assignment of the lease (i.e. transferring it to somebody else, so they become the tenant) will almost always require consent. This is usually subject to a duty on the landlord not to act unreasonably in deciding whether to consent or not.**

- **Sub-letting the property, in whole or in part, will generally require consent (except, often, sub-letting to other companies within the same corporate group as the tenant company). There may be other conditions which need to be complied with as well, in particular relating to the amount of the rent payable under the sub-lease, and its other terms. Provided any such conditions are complied with, the landlord will again usually be subject to a duty not to act unreasonably in deciding whether to consent or not.**

- Parting with or sharing occupation of the property is usually prohibited in the lease, with no provision for the landlord to consent, although again there may be an exception in favour of group companies.

- Lease usually separate out different types of alterations to the property, so that some types of minor work are allowed without any need to obtain a specific consent, some structural or external works are completely prohibited, and other works can only be carried out with landlord's consent, not to be unreasonably withheld.

- As to changing the use of the property, the position will depend upon the specific property. A lease for a particular retail use may well permit a change of use to another retail use, with landlord's consent, not to be unreasonably withheld. A lease of office premises, though, is unlikely to permit a change of use at all.

- Applying for any planning consent relating to the property is likely to be prohibited, or require landlord's consent, perhaps with no requirement for the landlord to act reasonably.

# CHAPTER FOUR

# WHAT MUST I DO ABOUT THE PHYSICAL STATE OF THE PROPERTY?

**This chapter covers the common lease obligations which deal with the physical condition of a property.**

We have noted previously that a tenant's obligation as regards the repair of the property may extend to the entire property, if it is the whole building which is let. That is usually called a 'full repairing obligation'. In the case of a multi-let building (i.e. divided up and let to several tenants), the tenant's obligation is restricted to its part of the premises, and is often referred to as an 'internal repairing obligation', which is a useful shorthand, though not always an entirely accurate description.

Whether full or internal, the repair obligation in a commercial lease usually places a higher obligation on a tenant than is found in a residential tenancy. A tenancy agreement in relation to a flat or a house usually requires the tenant to leave the property in no worse state than it found it, subject to fair wear and tear. A commercial lease will have no 'fair wear and tear' exception as such, and may well require the tenant to leave the building better than it found it, which can be an unwelcome surprise to them.

## Meaning of usual repair obligation

Repair obligations are typically quite short and to the point, and are likely to read something like this:

> *"The Tenant shall put and keep the Premises in good and substantial repair and condition, and replace and renew where necessary".*

If the property is let in a state of disrepair, the tenant is therefore obliged to carry out whatever work is necessary to put it into "good and substantial repair and condition". The required standard of disrepair is assessed by reference to the age, location and nature of the property, so while there is no 'fair wear and tear' exception, the tenant who takes a lease of a fifty-year-old property cannot be required to make it as good as new. Nevertheless, any disrepair must be put right, to whatever the required standard may be in the particular case.

The requirement to "replace and renew where necessary" is a recognition of the fact that elements of a building will simply wear out over time. The only way of repairing a rotten window-frame, for example, is to replace it. But there can be surprises for tenants as to how substantial an element of the building the tenant may be required to replace or renew. It may extend to major structural elements such as a failed roof, or to significant elements of plant and equipment such as a lift.

An obligation to repair is not an obligation to improve the specification of the building or component parts of it, so tenants are generally entitled to repair on a like-for-like basis. However, some repairs can only realistically be carried out with an element of improvement: if the rotten windows which are to be replaced were single-glazed, compliance with modern building regulations will mean they must be replaced with double-glazed units, and there is no doubt that that would be the tenant's responsibility. Similarly, the replacement for a thirty-year-old heating boiler will be an improved model simply because the technology has moved on: the new model will be better insulated and more efficient, and have smart controls. A tenant may therefore be required, within the repairing obligation, to effect some improvements.

This may even extend to putting right faults within the building which relate to the original design and construction: so-called 'inherent defects'. The case of *Ravenseft Properties Ltd v Davstone (Holdings) Ltd [1980] QB 12*, concerned a building constructed with external concrete cladding panels. The cladding had been designed and constructed without expansion joints, with the result that the panels came under stress when they expanded in warm weather, and they had degraded over time. The landlord required the tenant to install new cladding panels, but also to install expansion joints, which was clearly both an improvement and putting right an inherent defect.

However, the problem would simply recur if the cladding were to be replaced without any expansion joints, which made it reasonably necessary to install them in order to address the disrepair, and brought this element of the work within the scope of the tenant's repairing obligation.

There comes a point at which work which amounts to replacement or improvement, or putting right an inherent defect, will be considered too substantial or significant to fall within the tenant's repairing obligation, but it is hard to define exactly when that point is reached.

## Limiting the repair obligation

Twenty-five years is a significant part of the life of a building, and it might be reasonable that a tenant under a 25-year lease should assume responsibility for major structural elements. However, that is very hard to justify in a lease for five years or less. Increasingly tenants may limit their repairing obligations by reference to a 'schedule of condition', so that they are not responsible for any disrepair pre-dating the grant of the lease.

A schedule of condition describes the disrepair of the property at the time the lease is granted, and limits the tenant's repair obligation, so that it is not obliged to leave the property in any better state than that. Landlords may often agree to this because otherwise they would be unable to let the property without spending money on repairing the property themselves.

A good schedule of condition is a detailed, item-by-item description of disrepair, cross-referenced to good-quality photographs. All too often, what one finds is a few pages of photocopies of photographs which were of low quality in the first place. This is because the landlord has little incentive to spend money on having a thorough schedule prepared by a surveyor. Preparation of the schedule may be left to the tenant, and they too will often want to save money, and have little experience of what will actually be useful.

Even a well-prepared schedule may have restricted usefulness, however. If a schedule records, say, 50 broken or missing roof tiles, and at lease expiry there are 125, then the tenant's obligation is to repair the additional 75. Bearing in mind the labour cost and hire of scaffolding, this may make little difference. Or perhaps the schedule records that a flat roof is heavily patched; at lease expiry it is found to be in need of complete replacement. The tenant is not responsible for the complete replacement; however it is responsible for the additional deterioration. Its obligation is to give back to the landlord a building with a partially deteriorated roof, which is clearly absurd. All the schedule does in that situation is to provide a not-very-satisfactory basis for negotiating a contribution to the cost of replacement.

None of this means that tenants should not bother with schedules of condition. It is better to have one than not. But a schedule of condition is not a 'magic bullet', and tenants can perhaps think creatively about other ways of limiting the repair obligation, such as a financial cap, or an obligation to spend a certain sum per year on repair, or excluding identified elements of the building from the obligation to repair.

## Other relevant obligations

While the repair obligation is very important, there are other obligations usually found in commercial leases which should not be overlooked.

### Decoration

Leases will commonly impose an obligation to decorate, externally or internally or both, usually at regular intervals throughout the term (often every five years), and in the last year of the term. There is a significant overlap here with the general repairing covenant, since 'good repair' may include 'good decorative order' to a large extent. Nevertheless, an obligation to redecorate at a certain time will apply regardless of whether there is any disrepair.

### Reinstatement of alterations

Where the tenant has carried out any alterations to the property, there is usually a requirement to reinstate the alterations at the end of the term. Nowadays this is often at the landlord's option, rather than an automatic obligation. The practical issue is when such a requirement has to be notified to the tenant. Many leases do not set out any time limit, and the general view in such cases is that notice must be given by lease expiry at the latest. That gives rise to an obvious difficulty where the landlord gives notice before lease expiry, but too late for the tenant to be able to carry out the reinstatement. The problem for tenants is particularly acute where exercise of a break option is conditional upon performance of tenant's obligations, and the landlord raises a last-minute requirement to reinstate alterations.

It gives greater certainty for both landlord and tenant to have a timetable set out in the lease.

Compliance with statute

Leases generally shift onto the tenant the burden of compliance with any statutory requirement concerning the premises. This may mean that, for example, fire precautions works, disability adjustment works, even remediation of contaminated land, will be the tenant's responsibility, regardless of whether there is any disrepair.

## Anticipating problems when the lease is granted

In relation to matters concerning the physical condition of a property, the familiar rule is '*caveat emptor*' – let the buyer beware. That applies to tenants taking business leases just as much as it does to someone buying a house. It is therefore for the tenant to investigate the state of the property, and consider what that means in relation to taking on repairing liability. Investigations usually comprise two elements: a survey, and pre-lease enquiries.

Despite both those exercises having been undertaken, problems may sometimes be discovered even shortly after completion, when the tenant may find, for example, that fit-out works reveal the presence of asbestos at the property; or perhaps that the air-conditioning is erratic in operation, or the electricity supply needs to be upgraded for their requirements. In the longer term, the tenant may discover that even issues of which they were aware turn out to be more extensive in their effect, and more expensive to remedy, than had been anticipated.

Fee constraints on the surveyor may be one factor in this, but another can be that the urgency of completing the transaction overrides other considerations. A retail tenant, for example, may be desperate to complete the lease in time to benefit from the pre-Christmas trading period.

As regards responses to pre-lease enquiries, there is no obligation on landlords to respond at all, although if they do they are required to be full and frank in their replies. There may be an obligation to update the tenant, if and when the position as set out in their replies changes, running up to completion. Leases may contain 'entire agreement' clauses, which protect the landlord from liability for any replies, apart from those given in writing; this means, of course, that tenants must insist on written replies.

Particularly when a building is old, it can be a useful exercise for tenant, surveyor and solicitor to sit around a table together (and indeed inspect the building together) to understand the tenant's operational requirements, and the extent of the repairing obligations which the landlord is proposing, against the actual configuration and condition of the building. There is of course a cost to that sort of exercise, but set against the potential costs of repair at lease expiry, it can be money well-spent.

### Summary

**Repair obligations imposed on tenants by leases may be typically quite short, but can nevertheless give rise to substantial liabilities. They may oblige the tenant to:**

- **put the property into repair, if it was not in good repair when the lease was granted;**
- **replace elements of the building which have reached the end of their life, potentially including major plant and equipment such as lifts and heating systems;**

- improve aspects of the building, if that is an appropriate way of addressing the specific disrepair; and
- put right problems arising out of the original design and construction of the building.

Repair obligations can be limited by preparing a 'schedule of condition', which is a record of the condition of the property, and agreeing that the tenant cannot be required to put the building into any better state of repair than recorded in the schedule. This mechanism, though, often promises more than it delivers.

Other relevant clauses of the lease are likely to require the tenant to:

- decorate the property at intervals;
- reinstate any alterations the tenant has carried out; and
- comply with any statutory requirements.

# STEP-BY-STEP GUIDE FOR THE NON-LAWYER

This step-by-step guide is addressed to the non-lawyer, and therefore is included within Part 1 of the book, although Part 2 needs to be read before attempting to follow it.

It should go without saying that both tenant and landlord will have the greatest certainty that their interests have been best represented in the lease negotiation if they have had professional advice and assistance. If the lease is to be for a term of over three years, the law requires that it is prepared by a lawyer (see Chapter 7).

Assuming that the letting is to be for three years or less, and is to be documented on a DIY basis, this is a step-by-step guide to the process.

## 1 Tenant carries out due diligence

There are a number of points which a tenant should investigate prior to taking a lease:

- Will the landlord be charging VAT on the rent? This is at the landlord's option, and the impact depends on whether the tenant will recover VAT. If not, the rent is effectively increased by 20%.

- Will Stamp Duty Land Tax be payable by the tenant? In the case of a lease for a term of three years or less, at a rack rent, it is unlikely that there will be any Stamp Duty Land Tax (or 'SDLT') payable by the tenant. Calculation of SDLT on leases can be complex, and the best way to be sure on the point is to use the government's online SDLT calculator, at:

  https://www.tax.service.gov.uk/calculate-stamp-duty-land-tax/#/intro

However, broadly speaking, the annual rent would have to be more than £50,000 for this to be an issue.

- What is the energy efficiency rating of the property? The landlord is obliged to provide the tenant with a copy of the Energy Performance Certificate for the property, which shows a rating from A to G. If the rating is F or G, the landlord must not let the property.

- The tenant must have satisfied itself about the physical condition of the property. This may lead to an agreement that the tenant's repairing obligation is to be limited by a schedule of condition, and if so that will need to be prepared.

- The landlord should be asked about the title to the property. Does it need to have the consent of a superior landlord or a mortgagee in order to grant the lease? Does it have the power to grant the lease, and any necessary rights such as rights of access? Are there any adverse rights or restrictive covenants which might affect the tenant's use of the property? Ideally, the landlord would produce copies of its title, and of any documents referred to in it. These may not be readily understood by the non-lawyer, and of course this is one area where the tenant takes a risk by not instructing a solicitor.

- A solicitor would usually also make detailed enquiries of the landlord about many more matters of detail, and carry out local searches. Again, the tenant takes a risk if it decides it can manage without those investigations.

Realistically, these investigations are likely to take a few days, and should be completed before finalising steps 2-8.

## 2 Identify form of lease acceptable to both parties

What type of document?

The choice between licence to occupy, tenancy at will, periodic tenancy, and fixed-term lease is discussed in Chapter 6. It is assumed in this step-by-step guide that the document is to be a fixed-term lease.

Whose document?

Conventionally, the landlord draws up the proposed form of lease, and the parties negotiate any amendments to it. A landlord of a development with several units in it probably needs to use a common form of lease for all the lettings, to simplify management of matters such as service charge. In other situations, there is no reason why a tenant cannot propose a form of lease.

What form of document?

Whether using one of the three standard forms outlined in Chapter 9, or another form of lease, perhaps using the resources outlined in Chapter 10, the document selected must reflect the parties' agreement on the following:

- Will the lease be protected by the 1954 Act, or contracted-out (see Chapter 8)?
- Are there any break rights?
- Will the tenant have to pay business rates?
- Will the rent be payable monthly or quarterly?
- Will there be any rent review? If so when, and will it be on an upward-only basis?
- Can the tenant assign, sub-let, or share occupation?

- Will a service charge and/or insurance premiums be payable by the tenant?
- Who has responsibility for repairing the premises?
- What is the initial permitted use of the premises and will any changes of use be allowed?
- What rights does the tenant have to make alterations to the premises?

The Lease Code, discussed in Chapter 5, includes a template Heads of Terms which goes into greater detail than this brief list, and which could be of use. That said, much of that detail may not be relevant to a short, standard-form lease.

### 3 Make any changes required to form of lease

- Complete any blanks which have been left for inserting information such as the identities of the parties, the length of term, or the amount of the rent.
- Check the signature block at the end of the lease. A lease for three years or less should not be in the form of a deed (see Chapter 7).

  For an individual's signature, you may see:

*Signed as a deed by [name of party] in the presence of:*

*[name and address of witness]* *Signature*

*Signature of witness*

This should be amended to:

*Signed by [name of party]:*

*Signature*

For execution by a company, you may see:

*Executed as a deed by [name of company] acting by )*

*[a director and its secretary] or by [two directors]: )*

*Signature of Director*

*Signature of Director/Secretary*

The words "*as a deed*" should be deleted.

- If the lease is to be contracted-out, check the definition of the term. This will be something like "*two years from 25 March 2021*", but if it goes on to say "*together with any period of extension, holding over or continuation*", or words to that effect, those additional words should be deleted.

- Make any further changes required to reflect the agreement between the parties.

All changes should be initialled by the parties to the lease.

If the standard form used is in a file format (e.g. .pdf) which does not allow amendment, any lengthy amendments which cannot conveniently be written on the lease by hand may be typed as a 'rider', that is, a separate sheet containing additional text, to be attached to the lease. The lease should be marked to show where the text of the rider is intended to be inserted. The rider should be initialled by the parties to the lease.

If the lease will not be contracted-out, the parties can proceed directly to step 7. Otherwise, steps 4-6 must be followed first.

### 4 Landlord serves warning notice for contracting-out

As set out in Chapter 8, the landlord may wish to wait until the form of lease is agreed, and then attach it to the warning notice. Whether or not it does, the parties must at least have agreed the identity of the premises and when the term will commence, so that the form of declaration can be completed.

### 5 Landlord provides tenant with form of declaration

The landlord will fill in the blanks in the form of declaration, and give it to the tenant together with the warning notice, so that the tenant can sign and return the declaration. The landlord will have to decide whether to use the form of statutory declaration or that of the simple declaration. It will usually be the statutory declaration, and in that case the tenant must have the signature witnessed in front of an independent solicitor.

### 6 Tenant returns signed declaration to landlord

### 7 The parties execute the lease

Execution consists of the signature and dating of the document. The landlord signs the lease, dates it and hands it over to the tenant, while a further copy, called the 'counterpart', is signed by the tenant, dated and handed to the landlord. In that way, each has a copy of the lease, dated and signed by the other party.

a) If a simple declaration has been provided, rather than a statutory declaration, the execution of the lease cannot take place until 14 days after the warning notice was given to the tenant.

b) Dating and exchange of the two parts of the lease should not be done until the first day of the term, even if the parties have each signed their part before then (see Chapter 7).

Subject to the two circumstances in paragraphs (a) and (b), all of steps 2-7 could be done on the same day. They could even all be done in the same meeting, except that after step 5, if a statutory declaration is being used, the tenant would have to go to the office of an independent solicitor to sign it, returning to complete steps 6 and 7.

## 8 Deal with payment of any Stamp Duty Land Tax

See step 1.

# GLOSSARY OF USEFUL TERMS

| | |
|---|---|
| Alienation | A blanket term to cover all dealings with a lease, including assignment and sub-letting (see definitions). |
| Assignment | Transfer of a lease by the tenant to a third party. The tenant is referred to as the 'assignor', and the third party as the 'assignee'. Following the assignment, the assignor ceases to be the tenant, and the assignee becomes tenant in their place. |
| Break option/break clause | A lease provision giving the right to bring the lease to an end ahead of what would otherwise be the expiry date, by serving a notice. A break option may be something which can be operated only by the tenant, or only by the landlord, or it may be mutual. |
| British Property Federation/BPF | A representative body for landlords, which aims to sustain and promote the interests of those who own and invest in property. |
| Covenant | In a lease, the obligations undertaken by the tenant to the landlord are often called 'tenant's covenants', while those undertaken by the landlord to the tenant are known as 'landlord's covenants'. |

| | |
|---|---|
| Clear rent/clear lease | Under a 'clear lease', granted on FRI terms (see definition), the rent which the landlord receives is not reduced by any responsibility for the fluctuating elements of the property cost: repair, outgoings and insurance. This enables a ready calculation of the return on investment. |
| Contracted-out lease | A lease which the parties have agreed will not benefit from security of tenure (see definition) which would otherwise be conferred by the Landlord and Tenant Act 1954. |
| Deed | A document complying with certain formal safeguards designed to establish authenticity. Historically, a deed was sealed, and so a deed may be referred to as a document 'under seal'. |
| Execution | The point at which a lease or other contract becomes binding on the parties, usually through being signed and dated. |
| FRI | An FRI lease is granted on 'full repairing and insuring' terms, so that the tenant takes on responsibility for the repair of the premises (including service charge contributions), and the cost of insurance. These terms are the principal elements of the so-called 'institutional lease' (see definition). |
| Forfeiture clause | A provision in a lease entitling the landlord to terminate the lease in the event of the tenant defaulting on its obligations. |

| | |
|---|---|
| Full repairing obligation | In a lease of a whole building, a repairing obligation which extends to all of the premises (in contrast to an 'internal repairing obligation' – see definition). Although 'full' in this sense, the obligation may still be limited by reference to a 'schedule of condition' (see definition). |
| Group-sharing arrangements | Terms often seen in leases permitting corporate tenants to share occupation with other companies within the same group. |
| Guarantee/guarantor | A guarantee is an agreement made between A and C to the effect that C will perform obligations owed to A by B, in the event that B defaults. C is known as B's 'guarantor' (another term is 'surety'). In commercial leases, landlords often require that a corporate tenant's parent company (if there is one), or individual directors (if there is not), stand as guarantor for the tenant's obligations under the lease. |
| Inclusive rent | A rent which is the only sum payable to the landlord by the tenant for the accommodation; i.e. there is no service charge, and no liability to reimburse insurance premiums in relation to the property. The amount of the rent will be higher than if such other sums were payable. |
| Institutional lease | A lease on terms acceptable to an institutional investor such as a pension fund. Principally, it will be on FRI terms (see definition), so that the landlord will receive a clear rent (see definition). |

| | |
|---|---|
| Internal repairing obligation | In a lease of part of a building, a repairing obligation which extends only to the interior of the premises, the landlord retaining responsibility for the structure, common parts and services. The expression is a convenient shorthand, and the elements of the building which the tenant is obliged to repair may be defined in some detail. By contrast, a 'full repairing obligation' (see definition) extends to all of the premises. |
| Jervis v Harris | Most commercial leases provide for a 'self-help' procedure, whereby the landlord enforces the tenant's repair obligations by entering the premises to do the required work itself, and then claiming the cost of the work from the tenant. The effectiveness of this procedure was confirmed in the case of Jervis v Harris [1996], and so it is often called a Jervis v Harris claim, while the provision in the lease may be referred to as a Jervis v Harris clause. |
| Keep-open covenant | An obligation found in retail leases, requiring that the tenant remain open for business during normal trading hours. This can in practice be difficult for landlords to enforce. |
| Law Society | The professional body for solicitors. |

| | |
|---|---|
| Lease Code | The 'RICS Professional Statement: Code for Leasing Business Premises', which was originally published in 1995 as the 'Code for Leasing Business Premises in England and Wales'. The Code sets out best practice as regards the process of negotiating leases, and as to the terms to be contained in leases. It includes content which RICS members must comply with. |
| Lease renewal | The procedure leading to the grant of a new lease upon the termination of a prior one, under the Landlord and Tenant Act 1954 (see definition of 'security of tenure'). |
| Licence to occupy | A permission to occupy property, which falls short of creating a lease. Licences to occupy do not have security of tenure, and for this reason they may often be used to document short-term lettings. However, this is a risky option. |
| Peppercorn rent | A nominal rent, generally found where the lease is for a very long term, and the tenant has paid the landlord a substantial capital sum for the lease. |
| Periodic tenancy | A recurring tenancy, typically on a monthly, quarterly or annual basis. |

| | |
|---|---|
| Privity of contract | In general contract law, privity of contract is the principle which restricts the enforceability of contract terms to those who are party to the contract. In the landlord and tenant context, the principle is applied so that parties who have undertaken liability on the lease obligations remain liable after having transferred their interest in the property to others. For example, if a lease is granted to A, who then assigns the lease to B, the landlord can still require A to pay the rent. This rule now applies only to leases granted before 1 January 1996. |
| Rack rent | Rent payable at the full open-market rental. |
| Reinstatement obligation | An obligation upon a tenant, when the lease comes to an end, to reverse alterations which were carried out by the tenant. This obligation may be contained in the lease, or it may be contained in a 'licence to alter', which is the formal deed by which the landlord gives its consent to alterations being carried out. The obligation may operate in any event, or it may be at the landlord's option. |
| Renewal lease | A lease granted under the procedures contained in the Landlord and Tenant Act 1954 (see definition of 'security of tenure'). |
| Rent review | Periodic re-assessment of rent, to reflect changes in the rental market, and changes in the value of money. Usually takes place every five years. Most leases provide that rent can never be reviewed downwards, only upwards. |

| | |
|---|---|
| RICS | The Royal Institution of Chartered Surveyors, which is the professional body for surveyors. |
| Schedule of condition | A record of the condition of a property at a particular time, usually in the form of an itemised survey report with accompanying photographs. A schedule of condition may be prepared when a lease is granted, and the tenant's repairing obligation limited to maintaining the property in no worse condition than identified in the schedule. |
| Security of tenure | Protection given to tenants in business occupation of leased premises by the Landlord and Tenant Act 1954. A lease protected in this way will continue indefinitely unless terminated in accordance with the procedures under the Act, and even then the tenant will generally be entitled to a new lease, with statutory regulation of the rent and other terms. |
| Service charge | Charge payable to the landlord by all of the tenants within a multi-let building, where the landlord provides services such as repair and cleaning of common parts, provision of heating, light, electricity and water, lift services etc.. If the building is fully let, the service charge contributions of all the tenants combined should reimburse the landlord 100% of such expenditure. |

| | |
|---|---|
| Service Charge Code | The 'RICS Professional Statement on Service Charges in Commercial Property', first published by the RICS (see definition) in 2006 as the 'Code of Practice: Service Charges in Commercial Property'. This Code gives comprehensive guidance on the provision of information by landlord to tenant, the purchasing of services, the financial management of the service charge and more. It includes content which RICS members must comply with. |
| Simple contract | A contract which is not in the form of a deed, and which is executed by a simple signature. To distinguish it from a deed, or document 'under seal', it may be referred to as a contract 'under hand'. |
| Stamp Duty Land Tax /SDLT | Tax payable upon land transactions, including leases. It is assessed by reference to the total rent payable over the term of the lease. |
| Statutory declaration | A formal declaration, complying with the requirements of the Statutory Declarations Act 1835, which must be witnessed by a solicitor for a fee. |
| Sub-letting/sub-lease | The tenant under a lease may itself grant a lease to a third party, of the whole or a part of the premises. The original lease is then known as the 'head-lease', and the other lease as the 'sub-lease'. The third party is known as the 'sub-tenant'. The sub-lease must be granted for a term shorter than that of the head-lease. |
| Surety | Another word for 'guarantor' (see definition). |

| | |
|---|---|
| Tenancy at will | A tenancy which lasts 'at the will' of both parties, i.e. as long as they both want it to last. It can therefore be terminated on no notice whatsoever. |
| Term | The duration of the tenancy granted by a lease. |
| Turnover rent | Rent which is calculated in part or in whole upon the turnover which the tenant has generated at the premises. This type of arrangement is most commonly found in the retail, leisure and hospitality sectors. |
| Usual quarter days | 25 March, 24 June, 29 September and 25 December. |

# PART TWO

# DOCUMENTING A LETTING

Part 1 of this book, Chapters 1 – 4, was concerned with explaining the key content of commercial leases, and was written with the lay person principally in mind. This part, Chapters 5 – 10, is concerned with how to document a short-term commercial letting. It builds on the earlier content for the benefit of the lay person, but is intended also to provide useful guidance for the property professional, whether letting agent, surveyor, or lawyer.

# CHAPTER FIVE

# UNCERTAIN TIMES AND THE ROLE OF THE LEASE CODE

**This chapter considers the RICS Professional Statement: Code for Leasing Business Premises.**

## Background

Following periods of recession in the 1980s and 1990s, there was pressure on the government to legislate in relation to two specific areas of concern: (a) the continuing liability of former tenants under leases which they had assigned; and (b) upward-only rent review. The former concern was addressed in the *Landlord and Tenant (Covenants) Act 1995*; the latter, in the first edition of the *Code for Leasing Business Premises in England and Wales*, also emerging in 1995. Usually referred to as the 'Lease Code', it came into being as the result of a property industry initiative, designed to head off any legislation against upward-only rent review, in which it succeeded. It has been through various revisions since.

Bodies representative of tenants' interests, such as the British Retail Consortium, were also present on the Working Group which produced the Code, and the outcome was a consensus position on best practice in negotiating lease terms. It covered a wide range of matters, not just rent review, and came as a challenge to some established leasing practices.

As a Code, it has always been voluntary, not compulsory, and some landlords have been slow to accept its recommendations. Since 1995, nevertheless, there have been significant changes in what lease terms are regarded as normal or acceptable, as described very briefly in Chapter 1. This fact owes something to the successive editions of the Code. While its profile has never been high among small businesses, many professionals have made honest attempts to incorporate its recommendations where they could, so long as their clients were in agreement.

However, it is market forces which have principally driven changes in leasing practices over the past thirty years. Technology has changed working patterns and technical requirements in business premises, while putting pressure on bricks-and-mortar retailing. Environmental concerns have affected transport policy, with knock-on effects upon the commercial property market. Supply of commercial property has outstripped demand in many locations and business sectors. All this has enabled tenants to bargain hard for lease terms more favourable to them.

The Code remains a document which can potentially be persuasive when lease terms are being negotiated. From 1 September 2020, it appears in the guise of the *RICS Professional Statement: Code for Leasing Business Premises*, and it can be found online at:

https://www.rics.org/uk/upholding-professional-standards/sector-standards/real-estate/code-for-leasing-business-premises-1st-edition/.

(Alternatively, Google 'code for leasing business premises 2020').

It is essentially the same document as previously, though naturally with some changes, but now set within the RICS' professional conduct framework. This gives it rather more teeth, since agents (and landlords who are RICS members or registered firms) will potentially face disciplinary consequences for departing from the Code.

## Uncertain times

It is the misfortune of the Code's Working Group that this new document should emerge at a time of great uncertainty and change, and not only in relation to commercial property. It is a trite observation that business hates uncertainty, but over the four years since the EU referendum vote, it has had to cope with little else, at unprecedented levels, and in relation to entirely novel issues. Nor is the end in sight.

At the time of writing, the Covid-19 pandemic and associated restrictions on normal economic and social life are continuing. While opinions differ as to the economic impact (and of course the impact is global as well as national), it is universally accepted that it is major, and that the period of recovery will be of uncertain duration.

Quite apart from that, the retail and office sectors have been facing other pressures and uncertainties for some years, which have been intensified by the Covid-19 crisis.

Office sector

Flexible office space has seen significant growth over recent years, and the trend shows no sign of slowing down. This reflects a range of factors. Business plans are increasingly drawn up for short periods: a year, or perhaps a quarter. From the beginning of January 2019, *International Financial Reporting Standard 16* has required that lease commitments over 12 months be shown on a listed company's balance sheet. Employee working patterns have shifted significantly, and the enforced mass experiment in adopting home-working technology as a result of Covid-19 is likely to accelerate this trend. In this context, commitment to a lengthy institutional lease is highly unattractive.

Flexible arrangements encompass not only the familiar serviced office space arrangements pioneered by Regus, but also co-working, and so-called 'vertical campuses', in which occupiers may take one or more floors as core offices but also benefit from sharing centralised services and other facilities such as social space. WeWork and Workspace are established operators in that field, and while the occupier base has so far largely been smaller businesses, larger corporates are also beginning to use flexible arrangements. That is not only for their own occupancy, but may also be something they can offer in relation to surplus space to which they remain committed over a longer term, provided the alienation clause permits.

The reality for landlords is that they are increasingly having to accept short-term commitments by occupiers, often with flexible break terms.

Retail sector

As regards retail, the high street has been under pressure for a number of years. Major retailers entering into insolvency procedures has become a regular feature of the press. High levels of vacancies of retail units are there for all to see. Much of this has been to do with the challenge from online retailing, of course.

As in the office sector, shorter lease terms have been prevalent, to limit tenants' exposure. Pop-up lettings have been a feature of the retail landscape for some years now, and have become mainstream. Shopping centre owners Westfield dedicate space to pop-ups in all their centres worldwide, and they are used by luxury travel brand Kuoni and BMW (to promote its Mini brand), for example.

More flexible lease terms are therefore in demand by tenants, and in some ways also allow landlords to have better control. Agreeing to a break clause in the lease, for example, means that exercise of the break is something that can be planned for, in contrast to termination pursuant to a break clause inserted as part of a company voluntary arrangement, or by disclaimer of the lease upon insolvency.

**What is the market asking for?**

It is in the retail sector that there is the greatest impetus towards change. Issues which increasingly crop up in relation to retail leases are:

- Greater freedom to share space with concessionaires or franchisees, sometimes irrespective of restrictions in the use clause, thus allowing the tenant to freshen up their offer by livening up the mix of occupiers.

- Looser controls as to the permitted use of the property. The growth in 'experiential' retailing, offering customers the opportunity not only to shop, but also to enjoy experiences such as craft workshops, escape rooms and boutique cinemas, is a challenge to traditional use clauses. In the same way, leases might traditionally have prohibited public gatherings or overnight stays.

Now, overnight stays in an in-house 'apartment' have been offered by John Lewis, for example, as a means for customers to experience products. Public demonstrations of products, lifestyle classes, etc., may all be means to attract customers to retail centres. Experiences of this sort are something which online retail cannot offer, and so are increasingly valuable to bricks-and-mortar retail. For landlords, flexibility in use restrictions allows the tenants to create an increasing variety of reasons for customers to visit a scheme.

- Looser controls as to alterations to the property. Advertising has always been an important part of retailing, but now the speed and range of social media reaction mean that it needs to be more responsive than ever. In that context, tight lease controls on signage or public displays can restrict tenants' ability to undertake timely marketing campaigns to capture a trend at the right time. Also, businesses have had to react to the Covid-19 pandemic by making their premises Covid-secure, which will have entailed a range of alterations.

- More frequent, simplified break rights give tenants the flexibility they need, while offering landlords a higher degree of predictability in relation to vacancies, and perhaps the chance to replace a struggling retailer with a more successful tenant.

- Alternative rent arrangements are increasingly being tried. Turnover rents are an obvious instance, but even here there is now an increasing willingness to look at turnover-only rents, rather than the tradition model of a base rent with a turnover-based top-up. Variations on all-inclusive rents are beginning to appear, in which the landlord takes the risk of business rates going up and down, and other elements of the property risk such as the cost of providing services. Other models are possible, for example, rent based on footfall.

## What does the Lease Code say?

Against that background, the new version of the Code seems in some respects to run counter to current demands, and in others to lag behind what tenants are already negotiating in the market.

The Code is not a short document, but the following briefly identifies some of the more significant aspects it addresses.

- Break rights should be conditional only on there being no rent arrears, and the tenant giving up occupation, and leaving no sub-tenants or other occupiers. Disputes about the state of the premises, or what has been left behind or removed, should be settled later, as at normal lease expiry.

  *Tenants have anyway become significantly smarter at resisting onerous break conditions, and insisting upon breaks which can readily be operated. Breaks, too, have become operable at more frequent intervals, even in short leases.*

- Leases should require landlords to repay any rent, service charge or insurance premium paid by the tenant for any period after a break takes effect.

  *This provision is new in the current version of the Code, and it reflects the difficulty which tenants may face when operating a break, that they may end up paying for a period when they do not have possession of the premises. It is a welcome addition, although it might usefully have been extended to apply to all modes of termination. It may seem obvious that if the term of a lease expires, say, on 31 July, then the final quarterly payment of rent due on 24 June should be apportioned. In practice, tenants will pay an apportioned amount, and landlords will almost always accept that; however, it is not unknown for landlords to attempt to recover a full quarter's rent. A more general recommendation in the Code, that leases should not have the effect of requiring the tenant to pay rent for any period for which it does not enjoy possession, might therefore have been preferable.*

- Leases should allow either party to start the rent review process. Also, leases should not impose time limits intended to prevent a review, or set a new rent through inaction by either party.

  *This accords with present practice. Absent is the provision from previous editions of the Code that landlords should offer priced alternatives to upward-only rent review, which was the main raison d'être of the original Code. Here again market practice may leave the Code behind, as tenants are increasingly seeking flexibility in leases, and particularly as regards rent arrangements. Although the Code's authors cannot have anticipated the impact of Covid-19, this is really an existing trend which has accelerated as a result of the pandemic, and it is perhaps surprising that the Code does not at least encourage parties to consider alternatives to the traditional rack rent, FRI lease.*

- The new Code recommends that corporate tenants should be allowed to share premises with other group companies, provided they do not create a formal sub-letting, and that where appropriate, retail leases may allow tenants to grant licences of areas for use by concessions.

  *This is precisely the sort of flexibility that retail tenants in particular will be demanding.*

- While the Code recommends that alienation restrictions should generally be quite relaxed, it says that it may be appropriate for short-term leases to have more restrictive alienation provisions, provided they are reasonable.

  *There is no attempt to define what is meant by a short-term lease. The prevalence of terms for three or four years, or less, may therefore mean that the general recommendations of the Code on relaxed alienation restrictions will often not apply. This approach may well be at odds with tenant demands in such an uncertain economic climate, where they are likely be to looking for greater flexibility as to assignment and other matters <u>as well as</u> ever-shorter lease terms.*

- As in previous editions of the Code, it is provided that repair obligations should be appropriate to the length of the term and the condition of the premises.

  *Inclusive rents are increasingly seen, with landlords retaining responsibility for repair, and this may be another area in which practice is running ahead of the Code.*

- The Code recommends that control over change of use should be no more restrictive than required to protect the value of the landlord's interest.

  *Change of use is an area that tenants are likely to be very interested in, in the post-coronavirus economy, and they may want to take advantage of the recent significant relaxations of planning control in relation to change of use (the changes to planning law came into force on the same day as the Code, and could hardly have been foreseen by the Code authors). Landlords will be concerned about the mix of use within shopping or business areas, but will have to think carefully about the impact upon rental valuation and investment values if an over-restrictive use clause is imposed.*

- The Code makes similar provision as to alterations as it does in relation to change of use: control should be no more restrictive than required to protect the value of the landlord's interest. More specifically, a lease of an entire building should not normally restrict internal, non-structural alterations; a lease of premises within a multi-let building, however, may prohibit them, unless carried out with landlord's consent, not to be unreasonably withheld. In either instance, any alterations which adversely affect the character, value and structural stability of the building may be prohibited.

  *This is another area where tenant demands are out-stripping the Code. Emergence from lockdown has seen many occupiers needing to undertake alterations to their premises, to comply with social distancing and hygiene requirements. Retail tenants, specifically, will anyway require greater flexibility to accommodate the kinds of new uses, and more frequent sharing of occupation, which have been discussed previously.*

- As regards reinstatement of tenant's alterations at lease end, the previous version of the Code provided that landlords should notify tenants of any reinstatement requirements at least six months before termination. That always looked like a rather earlier deadline than landlords might favour, and the new Code is silent on the matter.

  *A good mechanism for obtaining certainty on this issue appears in the Model Commercial Lease suite of documents (see Chapter 10) and it could usefully have been adopted. In essence, it provides for the tenant to take the initiative, in the last six months of the term, by serving on the landlord a list of the alterations it has carried out. It will then only be obliged to reinstate those items which the landlord requires in its response, to be given to the tenant with a further three months.*

  *Much uncertainty and argument might also be saved by a recommendation that upon any alterations being carried out, the parties should agree: (a) whether the rent fixed at a rent review or a lease renewal should reflect the increased value of the premises as a result of the alterations; (b) whether the tenant's repair obligations in the lease should apply to the alterations; (c) whether the tenant is to be entitled to remove any item or feature included within the alterations at lease expiry; and (d) whether the tenant may be required to reinstate the alterations at lease expiry.*

- The Code makes no recommendation as to the presence in retail leases of so-called 'keep-open covenants', that is, an obligation to remain open for trade during normal trading hours. Tenants have had no option but to close during the pandemic, and generally speaking landlords have accepted that without difficulty. Such clauses are hard to enforce in any event, and there is a case for saying that they really serve very little purpose, and should not usually feature in leases.

- The Code is also silent as to 'Jervis v Harris' clauses, which enable landlords, provided the correct procedure is followed, to enter the premises and perform repairs, and then recover the cost of the repairs from the tenant. This process can operate harshly. Such clauses are principally there to enable landlords to escape restrictions on the enforcement of repair obligations imposed by the *Leasehold Property (Repairs) Act 1938*, and it might perhaps have been useful for the Code to recommend that in leases to which the 1938 Act does not apply (that is, leases granted for less than seven years), such clauses are inappropriate.

## Who does the Lease Code help?

It is open to question whether the Code will reach its primary intended target audience, that is, the small business tenant taking on a lease without the benefit of any professional advice.

All agents and solicitors will often deal with prospective tenants who are unrepresented. Small businesses tend to be very mindful of their expenditure, and engaging an agent and a solicitor to negotiate a new letting, thereby incurring fees probably going into four figures, can seem like a dispensable luxury. This is particularly so in the current market, where leases are comparatively short, and even more so if the property is a modest one, where fees in that order might equate to a number of months' additional rent.

It is increasingly not just tenants who are unrepresented. A landlord who may be marketing a low-value property every two to five years is equally unlikely to be happy about giving up the equivalent of some months' rent to professional advisors.

It is a mandatory requirement of the new Code that RICS members dealing with an unrepresented party must advise them of the existence of the Code, and recommend them to seek professional advice. In the previous Code, it was perhaps tacitly assumed that that would be done, but it remains to be seen whether the new explicit requirement will achieve any greater penetration.

A recommendation from the landlord's agent to seek professional advice may or may not change minds; it rather depends upon the urgency with which this is expressed, and how determined the tenant is to save money on fees. As to being advised of the existence of the Code, it would perhaps have been better to require that the unrepresented party be supplied with a copy of it, since having to seek it out online presents another barrier. The former Code had its own dedicated website, which was easily found, while the new one is not readily located amidst the RICS' sprawling online presence. Apart from anything else, having found it online, our cost-conscious tenant may not be happy about printing out a 42-page document (let alone reading it).

The previous Code aimed "*to ensure that parties to a lease have easy access to information explaining the commitments they are making in clear English*". It ran to only 15 pages, and was indeed as clearly and simply expressed as could fairly be expected. As well as being longer, the new document has no such explicit aspiration, and assumes a fair degree of familiarity with commercial leasing practice. It is not shy about using expressions such as 'wayleaves', 'security of tenure' and 'schedule of condition', which are likely to baffle the layman. The old Code contained an Occupiers' Guide which, running to 8 pages and 37 'tips', was daunting enough. The new Guide for Landlords and Tenants is an impressive encapsulation of commercial leasing practice, but fills 18 pages with dense text.

It has, in effect, something of a split personality: on the one hand it is a technical document aimed at property professionals; on the other, it seeks to equip lay parties with a degree of knowledge in relation to commercial property leasing practice. That is a difficult balancing act (as this book perhaps demonstrates).

At the same time, standard forms of lease are increasingly easily available for free online, and increasingly in use. While there has historically been strong resistance to the notion of prescribed forms of lease, standard documentation is used happily enough for construction contracts, and for domestic conveyancing, and in other contexts. It may be that one day a government with an agenda of removing obstacles to business will, if not legislate for, at least promote standard forms for simple, low-value transactions.

In Chapter 9, we will consider three forms of standard lease, and measure them against the recommendations of the Lease Code. It can at the least be said that having a statement of best practice like the Code represents a useful benchmark for lease negotiations. The lay tenant or landlord who has got this far in the present book will probably be undaunted by the Code, and will find it a useful reference.

## Summary

**The *RICS Professional Statement: Code for Leasing Business Premises*, while lengthy and in places using legal expressions without explanation, contains useful guidance on what can be expected from landlords in the negotiation of leases.**

**The content of the Code is discussed in this chapter, and it is a document which will repay careful reading. This book is intended to assist in following another approach, that is, the use of standard form leases, but it is suggested that the two approaches are best regarded as complementary.**

# CHAPTER SIX

# USE OF LICENCES AND TENANCIES AT WILL, ETC

**This chapter considers ways of documenting short-term documentation without using a fixed-term lease.**

To be certain of avoiding security of tenure, the landlord's best solution is a fixed-term lease, contracted-out of the *Landlord and Tenant Act 1954*. The common view, though, is that for a short-term, low-value letting, that is usually excessive in terms of formality and professional expense, since it will involve instruction of lawyers. This will be considered later, but first it is useful to understand the other methods of documenting such lettings which have typically been used, with the twin objectives of keeping costs down and avoiding security of tenure.

We begin with the licence to occupy.

## Licences to occupy

A licence to occupy is a contractual permission to occupy property. So is a lease; either type of arrangement results in one party in occupation of another party's land, and (usually) paying for the privilege. The difference is that a lease creates a legal interest in land, while a licence to occupy does not. One practical implication of that is that a lease is an asset, which may be bought or sold, or traded in other ways. Equally, that legal interest binds the landlord's property whoever owns it, so that if the landlord sells its interest, its successor in title is bound by the lease. By contrast, if a property owner grants a licence to occupy but subsequently sells its interest, the licence will be terminated by the sale.

Licences to occupy fall outside the scope of the 1954 Act (which is after all the Landlord and Tenant Act, and not the Licensor and Licensee Act). Landlords therefore sometimes try to avoid conferring security of tenure by granting a licence to occupy in preference to a tenancy. Many landlords and their agents have standard form so-called 'letter licences': one- or two-page agreements in letter form, which they use to document short periods of occupation, hence keeping transaction costs to a minimum. However, this is not always appropriate.

Following the House of Lords decision in *Street v Mountford [1985] UKHL 4*, in any dispute the courts will examine the transaction to determine whether or not the parties have actually created a tenancy, despite using a form of document which states that it is a licence to occupy. If the document is considered to have created a tenancy, then the tenant will benefit from security of tenure.

The key to the licence/tenancy distinction is whether, as a matter of fact, the occupier has been granted exclusive possession of the premises. It is 'exclusive possession' which is the factor distinguishing a tenancy from any other sort of occupational arrangement. The expression means: (a) that the occupier has the right to possess the property; and (b) that no-one else has that right. In effect, therefore, a tenant can deny access to the property to anyone else at all, including the landlord (excepting any access rights expressly granted to the landlord in the lease). A licensee's rights do not extend that far. If the occupier in fact enjoys exclusive possession, then there is a tenancy, regardless of what the parties have called the transaction.

In *Street v Mountford* itself, an agreement purporting to be a licence was held to have created a tenancy, even though:

- It was headed 'Licence to Occupy'
- It referred to the parties as Licensor and Licensee
- It provided for the occupier to pay a 'licence fee', not 'rent'
- It contained a clause providing that the Licensor did not grant the Licensee exclusive possession.

The court considered the reality of the transaction: it was a residential letting, and in any normal residential letting the tenant expects to be able to exclude the rest of the world from their home. The evidence indicated that that was exactly how the parties were conducting themselves: the 'licensee' in fact enjoyed exclusive possession, and the 'licensor' respected their privacy.

In the commercial context, while there is no consideration of a 'home', nevertheless the commercial occupier is likely to have cash, stock, equipment and sensitive data in its premises, and will therefore be concerned about security and will need to control who comes and goes. Most commercial occupiers will, in practice, have exclusive possession; a good rule of thumb is that if they lock the premises up at night, then they have exclusive possession.

Therefore, unless it is plain that the occupier will not in practice have exclusive possession, a licence to occupy is not obviously the most appropriate way of documenting the letting. The risk is that the arrangement might ultimately, in the event of dispute, be held to be a tenancy instead, under which the occupier would have security of tenure.

The situations in which a licence to occupy can appropriately be used are fairly limited, but might include shared warehouse space, or concession stalls in a shopping mall or department store, for example.

There are cases in which the courts have upheld the characterisation of a commercial transaction as a licence, for example *Shell-Mex and BP Ltd v Manchester Garages [1971] 1 WLR 612*; *Manchester City Council v National Car Parks [1987] 1 EGLR 75*. They have tended to be instances of agreements between substantial commercial parties, independently advised, and in such circumstances, the label which the parties have used may perhaps be given more weight.

*Clear Channel UK Ltd v Manchester City Council [2006] 1 EGLR 27* concerned the status of an agreement for the placing of large advertising displays. The Court of Appeal found that the agreement did not sufficiently identify particular sites and so did not confer exclusive possession of defined premises. This was enough to decide that the agreement was genuinely a licence to occupy.

However, in his judgment Jonathan Parker LJ suggested that a contract negotiated between two substantial parties of equal bargaining power and with the benefit of full legal advice should have the effect agreed by the parties:

> *"Where the contract so negotiated contains not merely a label but a clause which sets out in unequivocal terms the parties' intention as to its legal effect, I would in any event have taken some persuading that its true effect was directly contrary to that expressed intention."*

His remarks are quite narrow in their scope, and are unlikely to apply in the context of a short-term, low-value letting. As an example of that, they were considered in the case of *London College of Business Ltd v Tareem Ltd [2018] EWHC 437 (Ch)*. Tareem was the landlord of an office complex, and the College had occupied offices within it for teaching activities over a number of years. The occupation had been governed by a series of short agreements described as licences to occupy. The agreements contained the usual disclaimers that no tenancy was created, and that there was no grant of exclusive possession, together with a provision giving Tareem an unrestricted right to enter upon the premises at any time and for any purpose.

The court held that the agreement had created a tenancy, notwithstanding the express terms. The purpose of the document was to provide the College with premises from which it could carry on its business, and it was not realistic to suppose that the parties genuinely intended that the College's business should be subject to interruption by Tareem exercising a right to enter upon the premises.

The judge accepted evidence that the parties had very unequal bargaining power when the College first took occupation, and that the College took no legal advice on the agreement, so that the *Clear Channel* exception to the general approach did not apply.

The caselaw illustrates that there is no way that a solicitor can guarantee that the document which leaves their desk will effect a licence to occupy, no matter how carefully it is drafted, because the effect which a court will give it depends in part upon what the parties actually do after that.

One device which may be used to strengthen the impression that no exclusive possession has been granted is to include provision enabling the licensor to move the licensee from one location to another. This may be persuasive, but unless the power to move the licensee about is actually used, it may be argued that it is not a genuine power.

It is also true that a tenancy granted for six months or less will fall outside the 1954 Act (*s.43(3)*, considered further below), and so sometimes a policy is adopted of granting licences to occupy of no more than six months' duration. Where a licence is granted for six months or less, it does not matter whether there is in fact exclusive possession, and therefore a tenancy; the tenant will not have security of tenure because of *s.43(3)*. This works well, although one might ask why not call the document a lease, if it is one? Also, *s.43(3)* goes on to provide that if the occupier has accrued twelve months' continuous business occupation, then they will have security of tenure anyway, even if currently occupying under a tenancy for six months or less, so this solution is time-limited.

Despite the risks, licences to occupy remain in common use, which suggests that they do not cause problems very often. The serviced office sector, for example, relies heavily on licences to occupy. A certain amount of trust is involved, though, and the risks are real.

## Tenancies at will

A tenancy at will is a hybrid creature, whose legal origins lie in the concept of the licence to occupy. However, it is now a distinct form of occupation, a type of tenancy, under which the occupier has exclusive possession. Its essential characteristic is that it lasts 'at the will' of both parties; that is, it will come to an end immediately upon one party notifying the other to that effect. For the tenant, that may be an uncomfortably precarious form of occupation; the landlord can require them to vacate forthwith at any time. For the landlord, it is an insecure source of income, since the tenant can simply walk away from the property when they choose, with no ongoing rental commitment.

Tenancies at will are most often created by implication, in situations where the parties have not agreed upon the nature of the occupational arrangement, and a court is required to put a label on it in order to resolve a dispute between them. However, tenancies at will can be and are created expressly, and usually the reason is to avoid security of tenure under the 1954 Act. In the same way that landlords and their agents have standard form 'letter licences', they may also have standard form tenancy at will agreements.

It is established by caselaw that the 1954 Act does not apply to tenancies at will, whether arising by implication of law (*Wheeler v Mercer [1957] AC 416*), or expressly (*Hagee (London) Ltd v AB Erikson and Larson [1976] QB 209*). As with a licence to occupy, the courts will examine the reality of the transaction to identify whether a tenancy at will has genuinely been granted. It is easier to ensure a genuine tenancy at will than a genuine licence to occupy, though, since there is no need to avoid exclusive possession. Instead, the issue is whether there are any terms inconsistent with the notion of a tenancy which is terminable at any time without notice (*Binion v Evans [1972] 2 All ER 70*).

A tenancy at will must be determinable at the will of either party, and because the precarious nature of that arrangement is inconvenient and risky, the parties are often tempted to 'improve' upon it by agreeing terms which modify the position. The kind of terms to avoid, because they would be inconsistent with a tenancy at will, would include:

- a fixed term or specified minimum period
- a period of notice for termination
- a clause prohibiting or restricting assignment or sub-letting. This would conflict with the nature of a tenancy at will as a personal arrangement between landlord and tenant, which cannot be assigned or sub-let

- a forfeiture clause. A tenancy at will can be terminated forthwith, with no security of tenure, and so there is no need for a forfeiture provision

Payment of rent in advance *may* indicate that the tenancy is intended to be for a minimum term, or is to be periodic, and so *may* indicate that the agreement is not a tenancy at will. However, that is only one indicator, and so long as the document is otherwise unproblematic, a tenancy at will agreement can certainly provide for rent payable in advance. Where it does so, though, the terms of the agreement should provide for repayment of any sum that is attributable to a period after the tenancy is brought to an end.

Usually, the main objection to the grant of a tenancy at will is that it is simply unacceptable to the parties as a commercial matter to enter into an arrangement that can be terminated without notice at any time.

**Periodic tenancies**

Periodic tenancies may appear to give useful flexibility when documenting a short period of occupation, and to avoid repeatedly incurring transaction costs where occupation is extended. The problem is the application of the 1954 Act.

There is sometimes a misconception, as regards periodic tenancies, in relation to the operation of *s.43(3)*, which provides that tenancies for six months or less fall outside the Act. The sub-section goes on to provide that tenants who have accrued twelve months' occupation have security of tenure even if occupying under a tenancy for six months or less. It is sometimes mistakenly thought, because of this, that a periodic tenant has no security of tenure unless and until they have been in occupation for twelve months, but that is to misread *s.43(3)*. It applies only to tenancies "for a term certain", and therefore not to periodic tenancies. The true position is that a periodic tenant has security of tenure from the moment they go into business occupation.

In the same way, the ability to contract-out a new lease only applies to tenancies "for a term of years certain" (*s.38A*), so a periodic tenancy cannot be contracted-out.

It follows that a periodic tenant in business occupation must always have security of tenure under the 1954 Act.

## Six-month tenancies

As just discussed, under *s.43(3)*, a tenancy granted for six months or less falls outside the 1954 Act. At first sight, that appears to provide an ideal way of documenting a short-term let: proceed by way of successive six-month terms, up to the required total period of occupation.

However, the potentially problematic matter is the exception for tenants who have been in occupation for twelve months. The Act does not specify whether the length of occupation is assessed for this purpose at the beginning or end of the tenancy. Take the example of a landlord who grants three successive tenancies of five months to the same tenant. The first two tenancies are unproblematic: they are granted for less than six months, and the tenant at no time has more than twelve months' occupation. As regards the third tenancy, though, there are three possibilities:

- The tenancy is within the Act, because when it terminates the tenant will have been in occupation for fifteen months

- The tenancy falls outside the Act, because when it is granted the tenant has been in occupation for only ten months

- The tenancy is outside the Act when granted, but comes within the Act as soon as the tenant has had a total of twelve months' occupation

There is no caselaw to indicate which of these is correct. Some respected commentators have given it as their view that the third tenancy would be outside the Act, but nevertheless the only safe policy for a landlord who wishes to grant leases outside the 1954 Act is to grant tenancies of no more than six months, totalling less than twelve months.

## Contracted-out leases

It is possible for the landlord and tenant, by following the required procedure, to 'contract-out' of the security of tenure provisions of the *Landlord and Tenant Act 1954*. So long as the procedure is followed correctly, this gives the highest degree of certainty that the tenant will not enjoy security of tenure. The procedure is considered in Chapter 8.

## Summary

**A lease for a short, fixed term, contracted-out of the Landlord and Tenant Act 1954, is in the author's view the best means of documenting a short-term letting for both landlord and tenant. There are others, however, which have their place:**

- **A licence to occupy can be a short and relatively informal document, and it is common to use standard forms for this purpose. There will often be uncertainty, though, about whether the effect of the so-called licence to occupy is actually to create a tenancy, with security of tenure.**

- **A tenancy at will avoids security of tenure reliably, and again a short, standard form document will often be appropriate. A little care is needed to avoid including terms which might lead a court to conclude that some other type of tenancy has been created, with security of tenure. Also, a true tenancy at will is a very precarious arrangement, which can be terminated without any notice.**

- **A periodic tenancy gives useful flexibility as regards length of term, and avoids any expense or formality in extending the term. However, it does not avoid security of tenure.**

- **A tenancy for six months or less does not have security of tenure, though this is subject to an exception where the tenant has been in business occupation for twelve months. Granting a** succession of tenancies of six months or less can therefore work for a limited period only.

# CHAPTER SEVEN

# LEASE FORMALITIES AND THE THREE-YEAR RULE

**This chapter considers what formalities are required for the creation of a lease, and restrictions on preparation of leases by non-lawyers.**

As stated in the last chapter, a contracted-out fixed-term lease is the best solution for the landlord that wishes to avoid its tenant having security of tenure:

a) it gives certainty that security of tenure is avoided, unlike either

   *(i)* a licence to occupy, or

   *(ii)* a periodic tenancy;

b) it is not a precarious arrangement, unlike a tenancy at will; and

c) it is not time-limited, unlike the grant of successive six-month tenancies.

It has conventionally been considered, however, that documenting a letting by means of a short-term contracted-out lease requires the expense of instructing lawyers, while the other options do not, and those options therefore continue to be in widespread use. This perception is beginning to change, and the increasing availability of standard forms of lease on the internet has encouraged a growing number of landlords and agents to document leases on a DIY basis.

## The DIY approach

The residential letting market has of course taken a DIY approach to documentation for years. The residential tenant is usually presented with a standard form of tenancy agreement by the letting agent, and told "sign here". The document may be headed 'Assured Shorthold Tenancy Agreement', but technically it is a lease just as much as a five-year fixed-term lease of a shop or light industrial unit.

The usual course of events, in a residential letting using a standard form tenancy agreement, is that no amendments are negotiated. The letting agent cannot be said to be performing a legal function, just a clerical one. Commercial lettings, by contrast, are normally negotiated to some extent at least, and that makes a difference: an agent who has started with a form of lease and negotiated amendments to it has performed a legal function for which they are unlikely to have any formal qualification. It may well be that the agent's professional indemnity cover will not apply (though anecdotally some policies do extend to this). The difference, however, may be more apparent than real: using a standard form unamended may be negligent if its terms are inappropriate to the particular letting, and the selection of an appropriate standard document may also be a legal function.

There will, regardless of such considerations, continue to be pressure on agents to use standard forms to keep letting costs down, and leases documented without reference to lawyers are increasingly seen. Use of standard forms is not the only way of achieving a reduction in letting costs: some landlords have begun to use online processes, whereby leases of units within a development are concluded electronically, the process being similar to completing an application form.

Solicitors should continue to have a role, though. They may advise on the appropriateness or otherwise of particular standard forms, and the circumstances in which they should be used, or they may provide their own standard form of lease. There are required formalities which must be observed for concluding leases, and solicitors may advise on that aspect, supplying some guidance on procedures and also on what amendments to the form of lease might be entertained. Where solicitors have provided such advice, agents may perhaps be able to agree with their client that so long as they use the standard form, in the circumstances and following the procedures set out by the solicitor, no negligence claim can be made against them.

## Requirement for deed

Most leases are required to be in the form of a deed (which involves a higher degree of formality, and the witnessing of signatures) by *s.52(1), Law of Property Act 1925*. The law has historically applied this requirement to specified classes of document with significant financial consequences, including leases, as a protection against fraud.

The reasons for the existence of deeds as a feature of the modern law have been identified by the Law Commission as:

- providing evidence that the document is authentic, and was entered into by the parties;
- emphasising, through the higher degree of formality, that the transaction is of a nature which should not be entered into without proper consideration; and
- making it clear to third parties what type of document it is.

In the past, deeds were required to be sealed, and witnessed, and to be on heavier, more durable paper (originally parchment). The terminology used made a distinction between documents 'under seal', and those which were simply signed, or 'under hand'. In the modern law, the formal requirements for a deed, distinguishing it from a so-called 'simple contract' or 'contract under hand', are that:

- It must be in writing.
- It must state on its face that it is a deed.
- It must be executed in accordance with the required formalities. For individuals this means that their signatures must be witnessed. For companies, the options are: (a) affixing the company seal (relatively rare now); (b) signature by either two directors, or one director and the company secretary; or (c) signature by one director, so long as it is witnessed.

- it must be 'delivered' (hence the expression 'signed, sealed and delivered'). 'Delivery' of the deed is a slightly archaic concept, and does not mean physical delivery, but displaying an intention to be bound by it.

As regards practical consequences, the main significance of a document being a deed is that the right to sue for breach of the document's terms generally persists for twelve years from the date of breach, while in the case of a contract under hand the period is six years.

## Land registration requirements

Where the law requires that a lease should be registered at the Land Registry, there are prescribed clauses which must be included in the lease, and the Land Registry has its own requirements for establishing the authenticity of the execution of the document. It is only leases for seven years or more which are required to be registered, however, and so these additional requirements can be disregarded for the type of short-term letting under consideration, and fall outside the scope of this book.

## Non-lawyers preparing leases

There is a limitation on the extent to which clients or agents can adopt a DIY approach, since the *Legal Services Act 2007* provides, in effect, that leases which are required to be made by deed can only be prepared by a solicitor or licensed conveyancer, and it is a criminal offence for anyone else to do so.

The chapter and verse of this restriction is rather long-winded and tortuously expressed:

- Under *s.14(1)* it is "*an offence [for a person] to carry on an activity ("the relevant activity") which is a reserved legal activity unless that person is entitled to carry on the relevant activity*".

- *s.13(2)* provides that "*a person is entitled to carry on an activity ("the relevant activity") which is a reserved legal activity where … the person is an authorised person in relation to the relevant activity*".

- *s.12(1)(c)* defines "*reserved legal activity*" as including "*reserved instrument activity*".

- *Sched.2, para 5, sub-para (1(c))* defines "*reserved instrument activity*" as preparation of "*any … instrument relating to real or personal estate*"; *sub-para (3)* excludes from that definition "*an agreement not intended to be executed as a deed*".

- Under *s.18(1)(a)*, an "*authorised person*" is defined as "*a person who is authorised to carry on the relevant activity by a relevant approved regulator in relation to the relevant activity*".

- By virtue of *s.20* and *Sched.4, Part 1*, the Law Society is the relevant approved regulator for reserved instrument activity.

In summary: preparation of a deed in relation to real estate is a reserved legal activity; to be entitled to carry that activity out you must be authorised by the Law Society; and if you carry it out without that entitlement, you commit an offence. The effect of this is to restrict non-lawyers to preparing leases which are not required to be in the form of a deed.

The restriction is there, of course, to protect the public in accessing legal services. Therefore, under *s.15(4)* and *(5)*, there is an exception in favour of in-house surveyors. So long as a person (say a building owner) is not providing preparation of leases by deed as a service to the public through its employees, then if one of those employees prepares a lease by deed, for use by their employer, they are not carrying on a reserved legal activity, and do not commit any offence.

**Leases which are not made by deed**

Of more general usefulness, and of obvious relevance to the topic of this book, is the rule that shorter leases can be validly created by a simple contract, i.e. without a deed. That does not fall within the restrictions in the *Legal Services Act 2007*, and therefore such leases can be prepared by letting agents without any offence being committed. Under *s.54(2)* of the *Law of Property Act 1925*:

*"A lease may be made orally, or in writing under hand only, provided:*

*(i) it is for a term not exceeding three years;*

[A yearly or other periodic tenancy is considered to be a tenancy for not more than three years even though, unless determined by notice, it will continue beyond three years.]

*(ii) it is not of an incorporeal hereditament;*

[This restriction will not be relevant to a straightforward letting of commercial premises, and can be disregarded.]

*(iii) it is to take effect in possession;*

[The requirement that the lease must "take effect in possession" is best understood by way of contrast to the expression "take effect in reversion". Say a lease is to come to an end on 23 June, and both landlord and tenant have agreed that there should be a new two-year lease of the same property beginning on 24 June. They may meet on 10 May, and sign the new lease there and then, however it will only begin on 24 June, after the existing lease has expired. That is a lease which takes effect in reversion, since the landlord's entitlement to possession will only revert to it on expiry of the existing lease. If, however, the parties wait until 24 June and sign the new lease then, the landlord's entitlement to possession is immediate, and so the lease takes effect in possession.]

*(iv) it is at the best rent reasonably obtainable without taking a fine."*

[This simply means that the letting should be at the full open market rack rent.]

## The three-year rule

The principal requirements, accordingly, are a term of no more than three years, at the open market rent. They will be satisfied in relation to many short-term commercial lets. A little care and thought may be needed to ensure that leases are only granted to take effect in possession; the brief explanation above identifies the risk area.

So long as these parameters are observed, there is nothing in law to prevent a landlord or letting agent from preparing a lease without instructing lawyers.

## Application to use of standard form leases

The document used must be "*an agreement not intended to be executed as a deed*" (*Sched.2, para 5, sub-para (3), Legal Services Act 2007*, see above). If using a standard form, therefore, it will be necessary:

a) to delete any reference to the document being a deed; and

b) to check the spaces for signature at the end of the document, and in the case of signature by an individual, remove any provision for their signature to be witnessed, since this is not required for simple contracts. In the case of execution by a company, the execution formalities for simple contracts are the same as for deeds, so no further amendment is required.

Summary

**Most leases are required to be in the form of a deed, that is, a document which:**

- **states on its face that it is a deed; and**
- **is executed in accordance with the required formalities.**

Leases which are required to be made by deed can only be prepared by a solicitor or licensed conveyancer, and it is a criminal offence for anyone else to do so.

However, a lease can be created without having to be in the form of a deed, by a simple signed contract, so long as it satisfies these principal requirements:

- it is granted for three years or less;
- it is not granted in advance; and
- it is granted at full market rent.

A lease which meets those requirements can be prepared by a non-lawyer. It is necessary to check that the form of lease does not refer to itself as being a deed, and that there is no space for signatures of individuals to be witnessed.

# CHAPTER EIGHT

# THE CONTRACTING-OUT PROCESS

**This chapter sets out the procedures to be followed in order to contract a new lease out of the Landlord and Tenant Act 1954.**

The consequences of contracting a tenancy out of Part II of the 1954 Act are:

- It will terminate at the end of the term as set out in the lease
- It will not be continued under the 1954 Act
- There will be no right to a new lease

Contracting-out was originally prohibited, but was later allowed by amendments to the Act made by the *Law of Property Act 1969*.

## Procedural safeguard

While the decision was taken in 1969 to permit contracting-out, it was nevertheless recognised that the purpose of the Act is to confer important and valuable rights on tenants, and that there should be some safeguard to protect tenants against being misled or pressurised into agreeing to give them up.

The safeguard adopted in 1969 was that the parties should obtain the authorisation of the court to their contracting-out agreement, before they became landlord and tenant. In theory, and often in practice, this was a straightforward business. However, problems with the process emerged over time, and by the time of the next major re-examination of the Act, culminating in the *Regulatory Reform (Business Tenancies) (England and Wales) Order 2003 (SI 2003/3096)* ("the 2003 Order"), there was a sufficient degree of dissatisfaction with the old procedure for a new one to be substituted.

The present procedure came into effect in 2004. In essence, it is very simple. The procedure has three stages, which must be done in this order:

- The landlord sends the tenant a warning notice drawing the tenant's attention to the protection which it will be signing away;
- The tenant makes a formal declaration to the effect that it has read and understood the notice;
- The parties sign a lease containing the contracting-out agreement.

The correct prescribed forms of notice and declaration must be used. They can be obtained for free on the internet, in a variety of places, for example:

https://www.legalo.co.uk/template/property/declaration-and-notice-to-contract-out-of-lta-1954/

They are also included in the documentation for the British Property Federation's *Short-Term Commercial Lease*, which is one of three standard lease forms considered in the next chapter.

The notice and declaration must be exchanged before the tenant has become contractually bound – so for example, if there is a prior agreement for lease, they must have been exchanged before the tenant enters into the agreement for lease.

The layout of the current legislation is a little cumbersome, since some relevant provisions are contained in the Act as amended, while others are to be found in the 2003 Order. *s.38A(1)* permits the contracting-out agreement; *s.38A(3)(a)* requires that the warning notice be served in accordance with *Schedule 1* to the 2003 Order; and *s.38A(3)(b)* requires that the requirements of *Schedule 2* to the 2003 Order have been complied with (it is that Schedule which incorporates the requirements for the tenant's declaration and the contracting-out agreement).

**Tenancy for a term of years certain**

Before looking more closely at all those requirements, we will consider the effect of the provision in *s.38A* that it is only tenancies "for a term of years certain" which can be contracted-out.

- An obvious consequence is that a periodic tenancy cannot be contracted-out.

- Another aspect of the restriction was explored in *Receiver for the Metropolitan Police District v Palacegate Properties Ltd [2000] EWCA Civ 33*, where it was argued that a fixed-term lease which incorporated a break clause was not a tenancy for a term of years certain, and therefore could not validly be contracted-out. That argument was rejected by the Court of Appeal, and it is clear that the inclusion of a break clause does not prevent contracting-out.

- The case on this point which took most practitioners by surprise was that of *London Borough of Newham v Thomas-Van Staden [2008] EWCA Civ 1414*. For reasons relating to the old rule of privity of contract, leases often define "the Term" to include not only the fixed period, but also "any continuation, extension or holding over". Of course, a contracted-out lease would have no such period of continuation, so that wording would be inappropriate and unnecessary in such a lease. In the *Thomas-Van Staden* case, that wording had been included in a contracted-out lease, obviously by oversight. The Court of Appeal took the view that as a consequence the term was not a "term of years certain", and accordingly the lease was not validly contracted-out.

  There is much to criticise in the decision; nevertheless, for the present at least it remains the law. The upshot is that the definition of the term in a contracted-out lease should not include any extension, continuation or holding-over period.

## The warning notice

The prescribed form of notice contains a brief description of the rights under the Act, and of the contracting-out procedure, and warns the tenant that if it signs a contracted-out lease:

- There will be no right to stay in the premises once the lease ends
- The ability to stay there will therefore be dependent on whether the landlord is prepared to grant a new lease, and if he is not then it will be required to leave
- There will be no compensation for having to leave
- The rent under any new lease would be uncontrolled

A peculiarity of the prescribed form of warning notice is that the only information which the landlord is required to insert is the names and addresses of the parties. Other than that, there is nothing in the form of notice which assists in identifying which lease or even which property the notice refers to; there is not even a space for dating or signing the notice. In practice these notices are usually dated and signed, and since *s.38A(3)(a)* requires that the notice should be served in the prescribed form or "substantially" in that form, this is not problematic.

## Should the agreed form of lease be attached to the notice?

Under the old procedure, it was a requirement of the court rules that the agreed form of lease should be attached to the documents submitted to court. Under the present procedure, some practitioners consider it is still best practice to attach the agreed form of lease to the notice, to help in putting together the paper trail demonstrating that there has been an effective contracting-out.

This practice does, however, have the drawback that it resurrects a problem in relation to the old procedure which was considered in the case of *Receiver for the Metropolitan Police District v Palacegate Properties Ltd [2000] EWCA Civ 33*. In that case, by the time the lease was executed, the parties had agreed a number of changes from the version of the lease which was attached to the court documents, principally that rent was to be paid quarterly in advance instead of annually in arrears. The tenant argued that the court's authorisation must, under the Act, relate to an agreement to contract-out "the tenancy" identified in the court documents, and that if the parties entered into "a tenancy" in different terms, then the latter tenancy would not have been validly contracted-out.

The Court of Appeal held that the terms of the tenancy as eventually executed must bear a substantial similarity to those submitted to the court. "Wholesale changes", in particular changes material to the need for the Act's protection, such as insertion of a break option, might invalidate the contracting-out. On the facts of the case, the changes made were not significant enough to have that result, and the contracting-out was valid.

However, last-minute changes to documents are far from uncommon, and so a question regularly encountered under the old procedure was whether a change which the parties wished to make required a new court application. The decision in *Palacegate* was not of much help in answering that, although it did at least confirm the general consensus that an obviously minor change should not be a problem. The same problem might arise under the current procedure, in circumstances where the agreed form of lease is attached to the warning notice, and the parties then agree changes to it.

The problem may be avoided by not attaching the form of lease to the notice. Some practitioners will take the robust view that the current procedure is a complete break with the old one, and that since there is no requirement to give any information beyond the identities of the parties when serving the notice, the status of the agreement between the parties at that time must be irrelevant. Whether no draft lease at all has yet been prepared, or a draft is still being negotiated between the parties, or a lease is in finalised form ready for execution, should not matter. Equally, any further negotiation after that time should not matter: on this view, *Palacegate* is obsolete and can have no application to the current procedure. That is the author's view.

The more cautious view is that if the parties eventually execute a lease sufficiently different from what can be proved to have been in contemplation when the notice was served, then *Palacegate* potentially applies, with a risk of an invalid contracting-out. On that view, the best way of addressing the risk is to serve the notice with the agreed form of lease attached.

Anecdotally, there are probably more practitioners adopting the robust view, and not attaching a form of lease to the notice.

**When should the notice be served?**

Those who take the cautious approach of attaching an agreed form of lease to the notice cannot, it follows, serve the notice until the form of lease is finalised, or almost finalised. Taking the more robust view, the notice may be served earlier than that, even right at the outset, as soon as heads of terms have been agreed, and many practitioners are comfortable with that practice. Serving earlier has at least the advantage of giving more time to deal with any problems in obtaining the appropriate declaration from the tenant.

When contracting-out a short-term tenancy, which is likely to undergo little or no negotiation, there may not be much difference between 'serving early' and 'serving late'.

**The declaration**

The prescribed form of declaration:

- Identifies the parties and the proposed new lease
- Recites that the landlord has served the warning notice
- States that the tenant has read the notice and accepts the consequences of entering into a contracted-out lease.

## Simple declaration or statutory declaration?

The intention, when the current procedure was first proposed, was that in the normal case the tenant should have a 14-day 'cooling-off' period following the service of the notice, in which to consider the notice, take advice and consider its options. The contracting-out would not be valid if the lease were executed less than 14 days after that, and in any event would not be valid unless the tenant had made the required declaration.

However, following consultation, an alternative procedure was added, to allow speedier completions, but with a higher level of protection for tenants. Under this procedure, if the lease is to be executed less than 14 days after service of the notice, the tenant's declaration must be in the form of a statutory declaration, under the *Statutory Declarations Act 1835*, which must be witnessed by a solicitor for a modest £5 fee.

The rule is therefore a simple one: if the tenant makes a statutory declaration, the lease can be executed without delay; if the tenant makes a simple declaration, the lease must not be executed less than 14 days after service of the notice. One issue which had not been anticipated came before the courts in the case of *Chiltern Railway Company Ltd v Patel [2008] EWCA Civ 178*: if a statutory declaration has been used, but in the event the tenant executes the lease more than 14 days after the notice, so that a simple declaration would have sufficed, is the contracting-out valid? The Court of Appeal had no difficulty in deciding that it was.

The two prescribed forms of declaration are identical in substance, the only difference being that the form of statutory declaration has the required statutory formalities at the end of the document. Although the declaration is to be made by the tenant, it is invariably the case that the landlord or those advising it will send the required declaration to the tenant along with the notice, so that they know they will get back a declaration in a form they are happy with. This will be done even when the tenant has legal representation, but is of course even more important when it does not.

The statutory declaration procedure is invariably adopted in practice, for two reasons. First, the view may be taken that the notice and declaration should be exchanged at the latest possible stage (see above), so as to reduce so far as possible the chance of last-minute amendments, which might raise the spectre of *Palacegate*. That points to using a statutory declaration.

Secondly, even for those who do not take that view, practitioners usually see no benefit in using the simple declaration when that might delay completion of the transaction, particularly where the tenant is unrepresented and unlikely to spend as long as 14 days in negotiating the draft lease.

### Effectiveness of safeguard

It was never obvious that the old procedure of obtaining court authorisation provided tenants with an effective safeguard, and unfortunately the same can be said of the current procedure. It is a matter of speculation how much attention an intending tenant, particularly if unrepresented, pays to the warning notice and declaration. The process may often be regarded as just another tedious legal formality required before gaining access to the premises.

As to the statutory declaration, it is hard to see how this represents a higher degree of protection than the simple declaration. The tenant's solicitor, if it has one, will be unable to administer the tenant's statutory declaration, being involved in the transaction. The tenant must find another firm of solicitors. Most solicitors, administering a statutory declaration for this purpose, will wisely refrain from asking the tenant anything about it, much less advising them on the transaction. Tempting though it may be to help them out, the risk is of engaging them as a new client without any proper client engagement procedures or identity checks, and also of taking on potential liability to them in negligence. The risks are hardly worth a £5 fee.

Anecdotally, some solicitors in these circumstances do give advice on the consequences of the contracting-out process, and some potential tenants even abandon the transaction as a result – in such a case, it must be conceded that the procedure will have been an effective safeguard. But that is not usual, and otherwise the most that can be said is that having to make a statutory declaration in front of a solicitor may indicate that this is a serious step.

### Unrepresented tenants

Very many small businesses, on taking a lease of business premises, manage without legal or surveying advice, in order to save on fees. While that may expose them to being taken advantage of by professionally-advised landlords, it also gives rise to a practical problem for landlords.

The difficulty is simply that, even though it has been provided with the correct form, the tenant may not complete the declaration correctly (sometimes a problem even where the tenant does have legal representation). A common issue is the tenant just signing the declaration, rather than taking it to a solicitor in order to have it administered as a statutory declaration. If the tenant cannot be persuaded to complete this formality properly, then there is at least the option of accepting it as a simple declaration, waiting 14 days, and then completing the lease.

As regards any other errors, the landlord must insist that the declaration is completed to its satisfaction before the lease can be completed, and the tenant given access to the premises.

### Stating the term commencement date in the declaration

Unlike the form of warning notice, both forms of declaration require that some details as to the intended tenancy be set out. The only aspect of that requirement which potentially gives pause for thought is that the term commencement date must be specified. This is not always possible; it may be the date of execution of the lease, or it may depend on fulfilment of some condition, such as obtaining superior landlord's consent. All that can be done in those circumstances is to describe how the term commencement date is to be arrived at, for example:

- "*a term commencing on the execution of the lease*"; or
- "*a term commencing on the date to be inserted at clause [ ] of the lease*"; or

- *"a term commencing on a date to be agreed"*

Some have doubted whether that complies with the requirements of *Schedule 2* to the 2003 Order, but the purpose of giving the required information in the declaration is to identify the transaction to which the notice and declaration relate, and so long as the description used fulfils that purpose as best it can, then the contracting-out should be valid. That, at least, was the conclusion of the court in *TFS Stores Ltd v BMG (Ashford) Ltd [2019] EWHC 1363 (Ch)*. At the time of writing, an appeal is to be heard.

The requirement to state the term commencement date gives rise to further considerations where the term is expressed to pre-date completion. Assume that:

- the term is specified to begin on 24 June, but
- the notice is served on 8 July,
- the statutory declaration is made on 9 July, and
- the lease is executed on 10 July.

The first question that arises is: have the notice and declaration been exchanged before the tenant has become contractually bound? If not, the contracting-out is invalid.

That question has a straightforward enough answer: a lease operates as a grant only from the time of its execution (*Shaw v Kay (1847) 1 Ex. 412*), so the tenant's interest was not created until the execution of the lease on 10 July. The notice and declaration need not have been served prior to the back-dated term commencement date, 24 June, in order for the contracting-out to have been valid.

Secondly, should the declaration refer to a term commencing on 24 June, as the lease says, or to a term commencing on the date of execution, which is legally more accurate? It is suggested that it should not cause any problems to use some wording such as:

"*a term commencing on the execution of the lease, but calculated in the lease as commencing on 24 June [yyyy]*".

### Procedure and agreement recorded in lease

*Schedule 2* to the 2003 Order further requires that a reference to the notice and to the declaration, whether simple or statutory, must be contained in or endorsed on the lease. The actual agreement to contract-out may be contained in the lease, or it may be in a separate document, but in the latter case it must be noted by way of endorsement upon the lease.

In practice, there will be a clause in the lease, in standard form, complying with these requirements.

### Steps taken by solicitors or agents

If a letting agent, or a solicitor, serves the warning notice on behalf of the landlord, that would generally be considered to be within the scope of their usual role, and so they should not need to verify that they have the landlord's express authority to do so.

The position is different if the notice is to be served upon anyone other than the tenant itself: receiving notices is not considered to fall with the scope of the authority usually enjoyed by a solicitor or letting agent (*Re Munro [1981] 3 All ER 215*). Some verification of authority should therefore be sought, before serving the warning notice on them. Some practitioners will always serve notice on the tenant itself, even if assured that the tenant's solicitor has express actual authority to receive the notice. Most, though, will serve on the tenant's solicitor if assured that express actual authority has been given.

Equally, the declaration may be made by someone on the tenant's behalf, and if so then their actual express authority to do so should be verified.

It should be said, though, that the wording used in the prescribed forms of declaration recites that the declarant has authority to make it. The same statement usually appears in the standard contracting-out clause which will appear in the lease, and to which both parties will have set their names. This will generally make it difficult to challenge the validity of the contracting-out on this basis.

Such doubts as there may have been on these points have largely been allayed by the decision in *TFS Stores Ltd v BMG (Ashford) Ltd [2019] EWHC 1363 (Ch)*. In that case, a multiple retailer sought to establish that six of its leases, entered into with the same landlord, were within the 1954 Act, despite having in each case gone through the contracting-out procedure. On the evidence the court had no difficulty in finding that the tenant's solicitors and employees with whom the landlord dealt had the requisite authority to receive notices and make declarations. This conclusion must depend on the specific factual background, but it is likely to be very difficult for a tenant to succeed in establishing an absence of authority in situation where the landlord has dealt in good faith with the tenant's representatives who have been given conduct of lease negotiations and implementation.

## Problem areas

While the contracting-out process is generally simple enough, there are technicalities in how it works in relation to certain aspects which may be present in lease transactions. If any one or more of those aspects is present, the landlord will need to consult a solicitor, and a DIY approach will not be possible. The problem areas are:

- There is to be an agreement for lease, prior to completion of the lease itself
- The tenant's obligations in the lease will be guaranteed by a third party
- The lease will contain either an option for the tenant to take a further lease, or an option for the landlord to require the tenant to take a further lease.

Apart possibly from the second one, these circumstances are unlikely to arise in relation to a straightforward short-term commercial letting.

## Summary

**For a lease to be contracted-out of the Landlord and Tenant Act 1954, three steps must be followed:**

- **a warning notice is served on the tenant;**
- **the tenant makes a formal declaration that is has read and accepts the content of the notice; and**
- **the lease is executed, containing a clause which records the parties' agreement that the lease is to be contracted-out.**

**The steps must be carried out in that order. The forms of notice and declaration are prescribed, and are readily available online.**

**Some practitioners regard it as best practice to attach the agreed form of lease to the notice, and therefore serve the notice only when the form of lease is agreed; others do not regard that as necessary, and serve the notice earlier in negotiations. There are arguments for and against each practice, though probably the majority do not wait to attach the lease to the notice.**

**The declaration which the landlord requires the tenant to make may be in the form of a 'statutory declaration', which must be witnessed by a solicitor, for a small fee. If it is made in this form, the lease can be signed without any delay. Or it may be in the form of a simple signed declaration with no additional formality, in which case the lease cannot be signed until 14 days after the warning notice was served. The statutory declaration procedure is almost always used.**

**The form of declaration requires some brief details of the tenancy to be inserted; of these, the only one which might require a little care and thought is the description of the term commencement date, unless an actual date is identified in the lease itself.**

If the warning notice is to be served on a solicitor or other party acting on behalf of the tenant, confirmation should be obtained of their express authorisation by the tenant. The same applies if the declaration is signed by some party on the tenant's behalf.

If:

- there is to be an agreement for lease, prior to completion of the lease itself; or
- the tenant's obligations in the lease will be guaranteed by a third party; or
- the lease will contain either an option for the tenant to take a further lease, or an option for the landlord to require the tenant to take a further lease;

then there are complications involved in the contracting-out process, which require the involvement of a solicitor.

# CHAPTER NINE

# THREE STANDARD FORMS OF LEASE

**This chapter compares three standard forms of lease for short-term lettings.**

It was suggested in Chapter 5 that an alternative, or supplemental, approach to providing guidance in the form of the *RICS Professional Statement: Code for Leasing Business Premises* might be the use of standard form leases, to be used without amendment, or at least with a minimum of amendment. There is now a range of lease forms available on the internet, for free or at low cost.

In this chapter we consider three of them, produced by leading industry or professional bodies. These three should be capable, because of their provenance, of commanding widespread acceptance. The limitation on their acceptability is that these are not 'institutional' leases, and for a landlord whose policy is only to let on institutional terms these forms of lease will not be acceptable. Equally, if the landlord's interest in the property is charged to a lender, or the landlord intends to raise money on the property in this way, it may be that lenders will require any letting to be on institutional terms.

There is no formal definition of what is 'institutionally acceptable', but broadly it is a lease that is acceptable to an institutional investor such as a property investment company, pension fund, insurance company or sovereign wealth fund. It is important for all institutional investors that their assets are easily saleable, and are not devalued by the lease provisions.

The key features of an institutional lease are:

- It reserves a 'clear rent', meaning that the landlord is able to retain the rent and does not need to spend it maintaining the building or paying any other costs relating to the building.

- The other side of that coin is that it contains full repairing and insuring (FRI) terms, meaning that the tenant is liable to pay the costs of repairs and insurance, and may contribute to any landlord's repair costs through a service charge.

- It does not contain any provisions that would cause institutional investors to reduce their valuation of the property, such as obligations for the landlord to make good inherent defects in the structure of the property.

There is no definitive list of terms that are "institutionally acceptable". However, a good guide to what is and what is not institutionally acceptable can be found in *Schedule 5* to the *Certificate of Title* published by the City of London Law Society's Land Law Committee. This contains a list of lease provisions which are considered to provide adequate protection to landlords, and which therefore do not need to be commented upon in the certificate.

None of these three leases can be said to be 'institutionally acceptable'. However, the impact of Covid-19 and other pre-existing market trends may make landlords ready to consider letting on more tenant-friendly terms than have been usual. Moreover, when letting for short periods, landlords can perhaps afford to be more relaxed about the terms on which they will let.

Besides these three leases, other resources are also available, and some of these will be covered in Chapter 10.

**British Property Federation Lease**

The BPF's *Short-Term Commercial Lease* is available for free download at:

https://bpf.org.uk/our-work/research-and-briefings/short-term-commercial-lease/.

It is not sector-specific, being designed for "all types of property", and for lettings of whole as well as lettings of part. The intention is that it should be used for "temporary" lettings, typically a few months, possibly up to two or three years. The aim is to provide straightforward, industry-standard documentation, in plain English so far as possible. Other than five pages of introductory notes, and three pages reproducing the documentation for contracting the lease out of Part II of the Landlord and Tenant Act 1954, the lease itself runs to only six pages.

It is in many ways the opposite of the idea of the full repairing and insuring lease, and would certainly not be considered institutionally acceptable. However, the introductory notes say, "*The BPF is confident that landlords will be increasingly willing to offer*" such terms on a short-term letting.

Key features are:

- It provides for rent to be payable quarterly.

- It is the landlord, not the tenant, that has the repair obligation, albeit a limited one to keep the premises in tenantable condition. Even that may be further limited by reference to a schedule of condition. The tenant's obligation is only to use the premises carefully and not damage them, fair wear and tear excepted. This approach is very much in accordance with the Lease Code.

- While the landlord does have an obligation, in the case of a lease of part, to provide services, it is restricted to the bare essentials: hot water, heating, lighting, lift service and caretaking/porterage. There is no service charge.

- There is no obligation on either party to insure, and no provision for the tenant to reimburse any insurance premiums which the landlord may incur.

- The landlord bears the business rates.

- Such terms are consistent with the notion, set out in the introductory notes, that "*the landlord should be in a position to use his knowledge and experience of the property to produce a package which, so far as is possible, does not give rise to any unexpected costs to be paid by the tenant*". All landlord's costs are to be "*included within the proposed rent, which will remain fixed for the period of the lease*".

- Consistently with that, and as might be expected in a short-term lease, there is no provision for rent review.

- The document is restrictive as to alterations, having an absolute prohibition of all alterations, of whatever nature, including signage. That runs counter to the Lease Code's recommendation that control should be no more restrictive than required to protect the value of the landlord's interest.

- It is also highly restrictive as regards dealings with the property. No assignment, sub-letting or other dealing is permitted at all, the only exception being group-sharing. This is not actually contrary to any provision of the Lease Code, and indeed the provision for group-sharing is in accordance with it. Otherwise, the approach taken as to alienation reflects the suggestion in the Code that more restrictive terms may be appropriate in the case of short-term lettings. Since the lease contains a favourable break option, it is that rather than assignment or sub-letting which provides the escape route for the tenant who needs to offload the property during the term.

- The lease contains a relatively standard *Jervis v Harris* clause, permitting the landlord to enter in order to remedy breaches of tenant's obligations, at the tenant's expense. For tenants, a clause of this nature appears an unreasonable imposition, requiring them either to submit to the landlord carrying out repairs (which may often in practice close the tenant's business down for the duration of the works), or to undertake uncertain and expensive litigation for an injunction to prevent the landlord entering. Moreover, landlords may use the procedure simply to deprive the tenant of the protection of *s.18(1), Landlord and Tenant Act 1927*, which might otherwise limit the amount of damages which the landlord could recover for disrepair. The Lease Code, however, says nothing about *Jervis v Harris* clauses, and given the limited nature of the tenant's repair obligations in this form of lease, the relevance of the clause may in practice be largely restricted to removal of tenant's alterations.

- As might be expected, the lease contains the usual wording for contracting-out of Part II of the Landlord and Tenant Act 1954.

- There is a mutual break option on one month's notice. The option is not subject to any conditions at all, and in this respect the lease is more favourable than the recommendations of the Lease Code. However, it does not, contrary to the recommendation in the Code, require the landlord to repay any rent, service charge or insurance paid by the tenant for any period after the break takes effect. Tenants can mitigate the impact of this omission by paying attention to the timing of the break, as and when operated.

## RICS Lease

The *RICS Small Business Retail Lease* is not accompanied by any introductory notes, though it does come with a form of Heads of Terms. Its intended use is apparent from its name; it is retail-specific. Also, there is a brief footnote indicating that it should not be used for lettings longer than five years.

It can be downloaded for free at:

https://www.ricsfirms.com/media/1219/17005-rics-small-business-lease-inside-act-v2.pdf.

It is obviously a matter of interest to compare the RICS form of lease with the *RICS Professional Statement: Code for Leasing Business Premises*. It would be slightly unfair to list out the discrepancies, though. The two documents were produced eight years apart, and the Code is of general application, not restricted to short-term retail lettings.

Like the BPF lease, the RICS document can be used for lettings of whole or of part. It runs to six pages, and is in plain English. It is downloadable only as a .pdf file, not a Word document, so that in practice it cannot easily be amended. The other two lease forms are available in Word.

- Rent is to be paid monthly.
- As appropriate to a short-term letting, there is no provision for rent review.
- The tenant is required to pay business rates, unlike the position under the other two leases.
- The tenant has a repair obligation, though it is only to keep the property clean and tidy, and in no worse state of repair than at the date of the lease, as evidenced by a schedule of condition. That is in accordance with the recommendations of the Lease Code. There is a *Jervis v Harris* clause.
- Like the BPF form, it is highly restrictive of alterations, though it permits approved signage, and internal shopfitting, which can be regarded as compliance with the Code.
- Dealings are also very restricted, the only permitted transaction being an assignment of the whole with landlord's consent, not to be unreasonably withheld. As with the BPF lease, the tenant that wishes to terminate its commitment to the premises need not assign or sub-let, as it has the benefit of a break option. There is no provision for group-sharing, contrary to the Lease Code recommendation, and contrary to current retail tenant demands, which are likely to include flexibility on alienation.

- There is no obligation to remain open for trade during usual opening hours. As discussed in Chapter 5, the Lease Code is silent on this, though it is an issue about which tenants may have concerns, particularly after the Covid-19 pandemic and lockdowns. The RICS lease is ahead of the Code on this point.

- There is no service charge payable, though the landlord's obligations are restricted to keeping the remainder of the building in a state of repair such as will not interfere with the tenant's ability to trade.

- The landlord is obliged to insure, though the tenant is not obliged to reimburse the insurance premiums.

- Perhaps surprisingly, there is no provision for contracting-out of the 1954 Act. Given that the lease is only downloadable as a .pdf file, that may mean, if the parties do wish to contract-out of the Act, that a separate rider would have to be attached to the lease, or the contracting-out recorded in a separate agreement, the existence of which would then need to be manually endorsed on the lease.

- There is a tenant's break option, on three or six months' notice, which is not subject to any conditions. Like the BPF lease on this point, it is thus more favourable than the recommendations of the Lease Code. Also, as recommended in the Code, it provides for repayment of any rent, service charge or insurance paid by the tenant for any period after the break takes effect.

**Law Society Lease**

Model forms of commercial lease were published by the Law Society as long ago as 1994. Those forms did not prove popular with landlords, as they were widely regarded as too generous to tenants. In November 2017, the Law Society released its *Short Form Model Commercial Lease*, which is available in two options: one for a letting of whole, and the other for a letting of part.

The Law Society lease is intended for use in lettings of up to ten years, with one rent review. It can, therefore, be used for the type of short lets which this book is concerned with, but because it can be used for longer periods as well, it is much less of a departure from accustomed lease templates than the other two standard forms under discussion.

It can be downloaded for free, in both Word and .pdf formats, at:

https://www.lawsociety.org.uk/en/topics/property/business-leases-forms.

Like the RICS form of lease it is sector-specific, but this one is for use in relation to office premises, not retail. By comparison to the older Law Society lease forms, the layout is much more familiar, and the significant bias towards the tenant has gone. This document is much more balanced. Unlike the old forms, it is available for download in Word format to permit amendment.

It is a longer document than the other two standard lease forms discussed here, and this reflects the fact that it is intended for use by solicitors, and is not intended as a 'sign here' document. It states on its face that some tailoring will be necessary. Separate forms are available for lettings of whole and lettings of part.

- It has options for either quarterly or monthly payment of rent.

- Unlike the other two forms, it has no element of inclusive rent. It provides for the tenant to pay Main Rent, Insurance Rent and (in the case of a letting of part) Service Charge. However, the landlord pays the business rates.

- The tenant has a conventional full repairing obligation, though there is a drafting option for limitation by reference to a schedule of condition. Given the fact that it may be used for lettings up to ten years, arguably this enables compliance with the Lease Code recommendation that repair obligations should be appropriate to the length of the term and the condition of the premises.

- There is a conventional *Jervis v Harris* clause, and since the lease contains a full repairing obligation, this is more onerous for tenants than in the case of the other two forms.

- As regards alienation, this form of lease is much less restrictive than the other two, permitting assignment and underletting with landlord's consent, and also group-sharing arrangements. In this respect the lease complies with the Lease Code.

- There is provision for repayment of rent paid in advance for any period falling after the end of the lease, howsoever terminated (except in the case of forfeiture). This is in accordance with the author's comments in Chapter 5, and represents an improvement on the Lease Code position.

- There is a drafting option for contracting-out.

- There is a drafting option for a tenant's break, operable only at a fixed date, and conditional in certain respects. The conditionality complies with the recommendations of the Lease Code, however, both the other two leases are more generous to the tenant, the break options there being completely unconditional.

- There is provision for rent review, on an upward-only basis.

## Repairs, service charges and inclusive rents

As mentioned in Chapter 5, inclusive rents are increasingly seen, with landlords retaining responsibility for repair, and this may be another area in which practice is running ahead of the Code. Each of the RICS and BPF leases provides for a version of inclusive rent. They both depart radically from familiar lease forms. However, such ideas are not eccentric or left-field, but are being proposed by established professional bodies.

Whether such terms are acceptable to landlords will be circumstance-dependent. In the case of premises within an ageing shopping centre in a poor location, for example, landlords may be unable to let except on a short term, and subject to a schedule of condition. Trying to enforce repair liability at lease-end involves significant expenditure upon professional fees, and at the end of the day such financial settlement as the landlord receives is often not spent upon repairing the premises. Present structures thus often do not operate efficiently to secure the maintenance and repair of buildings. That outcome can be avoided by simply leaving repair and maintenance in the landlord's discretion.

As to service charge: if, in the course of a term of three years or shorter, significant work to common parts is required, a court may take some persuading that the tenant should contribute to the cost. In *Scottish Mutual v Jardine Public Relations (1999) EGCS 43*, for example, the tenant had a three-year lease with only a few months left to run when the landlord proposed to replace the roof. As a matter of interpretation, the court declined to read the service charge provisions as requiring the tenant to contribute to the cost of such a major item when its interest in the property was so limited. The tenant was only required to contribute to the notional cost of patch repairs to the roof instead.

It may just be realism on the landlord's part to negotiate an inclusive rent, rather than face the uphill struggle of enforcing traditional lease terms, when letting for a short term, particularly if the property is not in its first flush.

## Summary

*BPF Short-Term Commercial Lease*

- **It is not sector-specific.**
- **The landlord has the responsibility for repair.**
- **The rent is fully inclusive, so that the tenant pays no service charge, business rates or insurance premiums. The landlord is**

obliged to provide a bare minimum of services, but neither party is obliged to insure the property.

- It is intended to be used for terms up to three years, and so there is no rent review.
- It is very restrictive of alterations and alienation, though it does permit group-sharing.
- It is to be contracted-out.
- There is a mutual, non-conditional break option.
- It is downloadable in Word format, so amendment is easy.

*RICS Small Business Retail Lease*

- It is specific to the retail sector.
- The tenant has a repairing obligation, though very limited in effect.
- The rent is semi-inclusive: the tenant pays no service charge or insurance premiums, but does pay business rates. The landlord has a very limited obligation to provide services, and an obligation to insure the premises.
- It is intended to be used for terms up to five years, and has no rent review provision accordingly.
- It is very restrictive of alterations and alienation, and does not have a group-sharing provision.
- There is no provision for contracting-out.
- There is a tenant's break option, which is non-conditional.

- There is no keep-open covenant.
- It is downloadable only in .pdf format, so that amendment is inconvenient.

*Law Society Short Form Model Commercial Lease*

- It is specific to the office sector.
- The tenant has a full repairing obligation, though it may be limited by a schedule of condition.
- The rent is not inclusive: the tenant is also obliged to pay service charge and insurance premiums, though the landlord pays the business rates.
- It is intended to be used for terms up to ten years, with an option for one rent review (upward-only).
- It is relatively unrestrictive of alienation and alterations.
- It may be contracted-out.
- There may be a tenant's break option, conditional in some respects, but compliant with the Lease Code.
- It is not strictly a standard form, since selection between certain drafting options is necessary to tailor it to the transaction.
- It is downloadable in Word format, so amendment is easy.

# CHAPTER TEN

# OTHER RESOURCES

**This chapter outlines other resources which may be useful.**

It is worth making the distinction at this point between standard documents and precedent documents. Standard documents, such as the *BPF Short-Term Commercial Lease* and the *RICS Small Business Retail Lease*, discussed in the previous Chapter, are intended to be used without any amendment, other than filling in blanks left for details of the property, parties, rent and length of term. Lawyers are accustomed to using precedent documents instead; a precedent document is not a finished article but a starting-point. It presents drafting choices for different circumstances, and will usually be further amended in negotiation between the parties. The *Law Society's Short Form Model Commercial Lease* is somewhere in-between, describing itself as a 'template': there are drafting options to be selected, but the expectation would be that it would not be necessary for either party to negotiate any further amendments.

Few non-lawyers would feel confident about using a precedent document in the same way that a lawyer would, however many precedents for short-term leases are relatively simple documents which would lend themselves to tailoring into a standard form, for use in relation to a specific development, perhaps, or across a portfolio of properties.

## Lawyers' resources

This book has focused on three standard forms of lease, together with the Lease Code, and making mention also of the Service Charge Code. Lawyers will not be short of other sources of precedent lease forms, information and know-how, principally through subscriptions to online services such as PLC or LexisPSL. They will also have books of precedents to refer to, and will often maintain their own banks of precedents. In addition, certain clients will have precedent leases which are specific to their own policies, circumstances and requirements.

## Other resources

Non-subscription sites

There are non-subscription websites such as www.simply-docs.co.uk, which provides many lease precedents at low cost, including precedents for pop-up lettings and other short-term commercial arrangements.

There is now also a variety of free websites offering document assembly, so that a landlord can access the site, complete short letting details, and download a form of lease. Examples are:

www.lawdepot.co.uk

www.legalcontracts.co.uk

www.netlawman.co.uk

There are many others.

Model Commercial Lease

The Model Commercial Lease (MCL) suite of documents comprises various precedent commercial leases and associated documents. They are available for anyone to download from the MCL website, www.modelcommerciallease.co.uk, without charge.

Different versions of MCL leases are available to suit different types of commercial buildings such as offices, shops, shopping centre units and industrial/logistics units.

The MCL is intended to avoid much of the unnecessary negotiation on most routine letting transactions by representing a fair starting-point for both parties, but it is intended to be suitable for institutional lettings.

It is not designed as a standard "sign here" document, but as something which is negotiable, and it is unlikely that many landlords will feel confident about using it without legal input.

## Other information and know-how online

There are many sites from which guidance is available, for anyone wanting to discover more about commercial leases.

One point to be aware of is that some sites give guidance only on residential leases, where the law is very different from that relating to commercial leases. An example of this is the site of the Leasehold Advisory Service, www.lease-advice.org. If searching for sites it is always helpful to search specifically for 'commercial leases'.

Many firms of solicitors and of managing agents publish frequent bulletins, which are usually to be found by searching their websites. They are mostly either updates on new legal developments, or brief summaries of particular areas of practice. These may be helpful, though their usefulness varies widely, and they can be very restricted in scope. They are published, of course, not as a public benefit, but to attract potential clients, so that they usually stop short of giving enough information to enable the reader to do without instructing the professional.

Government guidance online tends to be general in nature, and understandably does not tackle specific problem situations that tenants or landlord may find themselves in, or discuss specific issues for negotiation when taking or granting a lease. It can be relied upon for accuracy, though, as one would hope, and a starting-point for finding out about many practical aspects of commercial leases is:

www.gov.uk/browse/business/premises-rates

A website which is addressed principally to landlords, but which may nevertheless have content which is useful to tenants, is Property Management Guide:

www.propertymanagementguide.co.uk

This site is very practical in its approach. Some of its content relates to residential lettings, but it is clear when this is the case.

# MORE BOOKS BY LAW BRIEF PUBLISHING

A selection of our other titles available now:-

| |
|---|
| 'A Practical Guide to Solicitor and Client Costs – 2nd Edition' by Robin Dunne |
| 'Constructive Dismissal – Practice Pointers and Principles' by Benjimin Burgher |
| 'A Practical Guide to Religion and Belief Discrimination Claims in the Workplace' by Kashif Ali |
| 'A Practical Guide to the Law of Medical Treatment Decisions' by Ben Troke |
| 'Fundamental Dishonesty and QOCS in Personal Injury Proceedings: Law and Practice' by Jake Rowley |
| 'A Practical Guide to the Law in Relation to School Exclusions' by Charlotte Hadfield & Alice de Coverley |
| 'A Practical Guide to Divorce for the Silver Separators' by Karin Walker |
| 'The Right to be Forgotten – The Law and Practical Issues' by Melissa Stock |
| 'A Practical Guide to Planning Law and Rights of Way in National Parks, the Broads and AONBs' by James Maurici QC, James Neill et al |
| 'A Practical Guide to Election Law' by Tom Tabori |
| 'A Practical Guide to the Law in Relation to Surrogacy' by Andrew Powell |
| 'A Practical Guide to Claims Arising from Fatal Accidents – 2nd Edition' by James Patience |
| 'A Practical Guide to the Ownership of Employee Inventions – From Entitlement to Compensation' by James Tumbridge & Ashley Roughton |
| 'A Practical Guide to Asbestos Claims' by Jonathan Owen & Gareth McAloon |
| 'A Practical Guide to Stamp Duty Land Tax in England and Northern Ireland' by Suzanne O'Hara |
| 'A Practical Guide to the Law of Farming Partnerships' by Philip Whitcomb |

| |
|---|
| 'Covid-19, Homeworking and the Law – The Essential Guide to Employment and GDPR Issues' by Forbes Solicitors |
| 'Covid-19, Force Majeure and Frustration of Contracts – The Essential Guide' by Keith Markham |
| 'Covid-19 and Criminal Law – The Essential Guide' by Ramya Nagesh |
| 'Covid-19 and Family Law in England and Wales – The Essential Guide' by Safda Mahmood |
| 'A Practical Guide to the Law of Unlawful Eviction and Harassment – 2nd Edition' by Stephanie Lovegrove |
| 'Covid-19, Residential Property, Equity Release and Enfranchisement – The Essential Guide' by Paul Sams and Louise Uphill |
| 'Covid-19, Brexit and the Law of Commercial Leases – The Essential Guide' by Mark Shelton |
| 'A Practical Guide to Costs in Personal Injury Claims – 2nd Edition' by Matthew Hoe |
| 'A Practical Guide to the General Data Protection Regulation (GDPR) – 2nd Edition' by Keith Markham |
| 'Ellis on Credit Hire – Sixth Edition' by Aidan Ellis & Tim Kevan |
| 'A Practical Guide to Working with Litigants in Person and McKenzie Friends in Family Cases' by Stuart Barlow |
| 'Protecting Unregistered Brands: A Practical Guide to the Law of Passing Off' by Lorna Brazell |
| 'A Practical Guide to Secondary Liability and Joint Enterprise Post-Jogee' by Joanne Cecil & James Mehigan |
| 'A Practical Guide to the Pre-Action RTA Claims Protocol for Personal Injury Lawyers' by Antonia Ford |
| 'A Practical Guide to Neighbour Disputes and the Law' by Alexander Walsh |
| 'A Practical Guide to Forfeiture of Leases' by Mark Shelton |
| 'A Practical Guide to Coercive Control for Legal Practitioners and Victims' by Rachel Horman |

| |
|---|
| 'A Practical Guide to Rights Over Airspace and Subsoil' by Daniel Gatty |
| 'Tackling Disclosure in the Criminal Courts – A Practitioner's Guide' by Narita Bahra QC & Don Ramble |
| 'A Practical Guide to the Law of Driverless Cars – Second Edition' by Alex Glassbrook, Emma Northey & Scarlett Milligan |
| 'A Practical Guide to TOLATA Claims' by Greg Williams |
| 'Artificial Intelligence – The Practical Legal Issues' by John Buyers |
| 'A Practical Guide to the Law of Prescription in Scotland' by Andrew Foyle |
| 'A Practical Guide to the Construction and Rectification of Wills and Trust Instruments' by Edward Hewitt |
| 'A Practical Guide to the Law of Bullying and Harassment in the Workplace' by Philip Hyland |
| 'How to Be a Freelance Solicitor: A Practical Guide to the SRA-Regulated Freelance Solicitor Model' by Paul Bennett |
| 'A Practical Guide to Prison Injury Claims' by Malcolm Johnson |
| 'A Practical Guide to the Small Claims Track' by Dominic Bright |
| 'A Practical Guide to Advising Clients at the Police Station' by Colin Stephen McKeown-Beaumont |
| 'A Practical Guide to Antisocial Behaviour Injunctions' by Iain Wightwick |
| 'Practical Mediation: A Guide for Mediators, Advocates, Advisers, Lawyers, and Students in Civil, Commercial, Business, Property, Workplace, and Employment Cases' by Jonathan Dingle with John Sephton |
| 'The Mini-Pupillage Workbook' by David Boyle |
| 'A Practical Guide to Crofting Law' by Brian Inkster |
| 'A Practical Guide to Spousal Maintenance' by Liz Cowell |
| 'A Practical Guide to the Law of Domain Names and Cybersquatting' by Andrew Clemson |
| 'A Practical Guide to the Law of Gender Pay Gap Reporting' by Harini Iyengar |

'A Practical Guide to the Rights of Grandparents in Children Proceedings' by Stuart Barlow

'NHS Whistleblowing and the Law' by Joseph England

'Employment Law and the Gig Economy' by Nigel Mackay & Annie Powell

'A Practical Guide to Noise Induced Hearing Loss (NIHL) Claims' by Andrew Mckie, Ian Skeate, Gareth McAloon

'An Introduction to Beauty Negligence Claims – A Practical Guide for the Personal Injury Practitioner' by Greg Almond

'Intercompany Agreements for Transfer Pricing Compliance' by Paul Sutton

'Zen and the Art of Mediation' by Martin Plowman

'A Practical Guide to the SRA Principles, Individual and Law Firm Codes of Conduct 2019 – What Every Law Firm Needs to Know' by Paul Bennett

'A Practical Guide to Adoption for Family Lawyers' by Graham Pegg

'A Practical Guide to Industrial Disease Claims' by Andrew Mckie & Ian Skeate

'A Practical Guide to Redundancy' by Philip Hyland

'A Practical Guide to Vicarious Liability' by Mariel Irvine

'A Practical Guide to Applications for Landlord's Consent and Variation of Leases' by Mark Shelton

'A Practical Guide to Relief from Sanctions Post-Mitchell and Denton' by Peter Causton

'A Practical Guide to Equity Release for Advisors' by Paul Sams

'A Practical Guide to the Law Relating to Food' by Ian Thomas

'A Practical Guide to Financial Services Claims' by Chris Hegarty

'The Law of Houses in Multiple Occupation: A Practical Guide to HMO Proceedings' by Julian Hunt

'A Practical Guide to Unlawful Eviction and Harassment' by Stephanie Lovegrove

'Occupiers, Highways and Defective Premises Claims: A Practical Guide Post-Jackson – 2nd Edition' by Andrew Mckie

| |
|---|
| ‘A Practical Guide to Financial Ombudsman Service Claims’ by Adam Temple & Robert Scrivenor |
| 'A Practical Guide to Advising Schools on Employment Law' by Jonathan Holden |
| ‘A Practical Guide to Running Housing Disrepair and Cavity Wall Claims: 2nd Edition’ by Andrew Mckie & Ian Skeate |
| ‘A Practical Guide to Holiday Sickness Claims – 2nd Edition’ by Andrew Mckie & Ian Skeate |
| ‘Arguments and Tactics for Personal Injury and Clinical Negligence Claims’ by Dorian Williams |
| ‘A Practical Guide to Drone Law’ by Rufus Ballaster, Andrew Firman, Eleanor Clot |
| ‘A Practical Guide to Compliance for Personal Injury Firms Working With Claims Management Companies’ by Paul Bennett |
| ‘A Practical Guide to Dog Law for Owners and Others’ by Andrea Pitt |
| ‘RTA Allegations of Fraud in a Post-Jackson Era: The Handbook – 2nd Edition’ by Andrew Mckie |
| ‘RTA Personal Injury Claims: A Practical Guide Post-Jackson’ by Andrew Mckie |
| ‘On Experts: CPR35 for Lawyers and Experts’ by David Boyle |
| ‘An Introduction to Personal Injury Law’ by David Boyle |
| ‘A Practical Guide to Subtle Brain Injury Claims’ by Pankaj Madan |

These books and more are available to order online direct from the publisher at www.lawbriefpublishing.com, where you can also read free sample chapters. For any queries, contact us on 0844 587 2383 or mail@lawbriefpublishing.com.

Our books are also usually in stock at www.amazon.co.uk with free next day delivery for Prime members, and at good legal bookshops such as Wildy & Sons.

We are regularly launching new books in our series of practical day-to-day practitioners' guides. Visit our website and join our free newsletter to be kept informed and to receive special offers, free chapters, etc.

You can also follow us on Twitter at www.twitter.com/lawbriefpub.

www.ingramcontent.com/pod-product-compliance
Lightning Source LLC
LaVergne TN
LVHW022100200926
848481LV00003B/997